THE JOY OF GARDENING

VANESSA BERRIDGE

summersdale

Summersdale Publishers Ltd
46 West Street
Chichester
West Sussex
PO19 1RP
UK

www.summersdale.com

Printed and bound in the Czech Republic

ISBN: 978-1-84953-552-6

Substantial discounts on bulk quantities of Summersdale books are available to corporations, professional associations and other organisations. For details contact Nicky Douglas by telephone: +44 (0) 1243 756902, fax: +44 (0) 1243 786300 or email: nicky@summersdale.com.

In memory of Norman Berridge

CONTENTS

INTRODUCTION

If you have a garden and a library, you have everything you need.
CICERO (103–43BCE)

Gardening is addictive. People will say they've played squash, frequented the gym, or taken up painting for a while, but you never, ever hear anyone say that they had gardened for a couple of years and then given it up, because nobody ever does. Once a gardener, always a gardener. Once hooked, you won't pass a garden centre, a plant nursery or one of those yellow signs saying 'Garden Open Today', without plunging in to buy yet another plant or to admire other people's hard work.

Gardens and gardening continue to grow in popularity. The figures prove it: membership of the

Royal Horticultural Society, Britain's leading garden charity, has almost trebled in the last twenty years to over 400,000. The number of private gardens opening for charity under the National Gardens Scheme increases annually, while visiting a garden centre is now one of the most popular leisure activities in the UK. And, at the beginning of the twenty-first century, waiting lists for allotments have never been longer.

Consider, too, new plants constantly being propagated. The *RHS Plant Finder*, the annual bible for any gardener, listed some 50,000 plants in an early 1990s edition: it now contains more than 70,000.

So what is the allure of an activity which can be frustrating, bad for your hands, back and knees, and cause the ruination of your hair? It may seem a cliché, but it's true: gardening is an antidote to the fast pace of modern life. What could be more restorative on a summer's evening after a tiresome day in the office and a hot, sticky journey home, than going outside to water and deadhead, and enjoy the fruits of your labours?

Gardening, at least in Britain, is about custom and practice. A love of nature, and, in particular, of its cultivation, is part of the British consciousness. The pastoral theme runs like a river through English literature: Shakespeare, Milton, Keats and Wordsworth all wrote about gardens. Most of us, whether we're aware of it or not, garden within some kind of tradition. We reach back to an imagined prelapsarian cottage-garden past by mixing flowers with vegetables, to the grandeur of the eighteenth century by laying wide lawns, to the formality of the Elizabethan garden by planting out a box-edged knot garden, or to the post-war horticultural shows by reintroducing rows of dahlias to the border.

It is thought that 90 per cent of UK households have somewhere they can grow outdoor plants, even if it's only a window box. If you travel into London by train and look out of the carriage window, you will see, squeezed up against railway embankments, sunless backyards which still manage a brave display of colours.

For most gardeners, the fascination lies in the very fact you can't control nature; that, however hard you try, it will always outsmart you. The element of surprise - a foxglove reappearing after two years, cranesbills turning up where you least expect to find them, a rose flowering again after hard pruning and a year's rest - is fundamental, too.

Gardening is unhurried, and needs patience. The now prevalent idea that gardening is about a quick fix and an immediately pleasing prospect is not one which is subscribed to by keen gardeners. They actually like being outside in all weathers - repairing storm damage or sweeping up leaves. They are happy to defy the wintry cold to spot the first snowdrops at the bottom of the garden. They enjoy watching their herbaceous plants come through and spending afternoons staking them. Gardening is not just a job for the summer: many of the toughest jobs have to be done in the autumn and winter. But winter is also a time for planning, for reading catalogues and ordering new plants on a cold evening in expectation of summer delights. A list of

plant names is enough to give most gardeners a thrill of pleasure and to provide a vision of a floral future.

This book aims to throw light on the wonderful world of gardening, and to explain its perennial appeal. It will delve into the history of gardens and gardening. Different types of garden will be explored, as will the development of gardening tools, from the humble wooden dibber to the highly sophisticated robomower. Readers will be introduced to gardeners down the centuries, from an ancient Greek botanist to the television stars of today. Other people's gardens, large and small, are the chief inspiration for every gardener, so no book about the joy of gardening would be complete without a visit to some of the world's most important and fascinating gardens. There's a competitive edge, too, to gardening. This spans the individual gardener's endeavour to grow the longest, straightest courgette for the local village show, to the frenzied attempts to win Best in Show at the Chelsea Flower Show, where gardens can cost in excess of £200,000. And where would gardens be without flowers? We turn finally to the naming of plants and the language of flowers.

The intention is to introduce the beginner to the intoxicating effect of gardens and gardening, and to confirm in the garden lover the unparalleled delights of this very special human endeavour.

CHAPTER 1

A BRIEF HISTORY OF GARDENING

The many great gardens of the world… all make the point as clear as possible: The soul cannot thrive in the absence of a garden. If you don't want paradise, you are not human; and if you are not human, you don't have a soul.

Sir Thomas More (1478–1535)

In the beginning

In the beginning, God gave man a garden and, you could say, from thence all our troubles flow. The serpent beguiled Eve, then she and Adam got a taste for knowledge but also a blast of cold air as God slung them out of Paradise to till the soil elsewhere. It was an inauspicious start, but that original Garden of Eden put gardening on the map and invested gardens with potent symbolism used by writers, politicians and image-makers ever since.

Away from the myth

Moving on from Biblical myth, where did gardening really start? For many, it's now a leisure activity, but it took thousands of years for horticulture to reach that point. Our prehistoric forebears began gardening by harvesting fruit in forests. Then, by about 10,000BCE, they were cutting down trees, and enclosing land to keep out wild animals and marauders. Within these enclosures, they tilled the ground and sowed crops, as is suggested by Neolithic, Bronze Age and Iron Age field patterns in East Anglia.

Middle Eastern matters

Sumerian tribes irrigated the land between the Tigris and Euphrates rivers in about 3,000BCE. Mesopotamia (present-day Iran) was the site of the mythical Garden of Eden and the Hanging Gardens of Babylon. The Hanging Gardens, one of the Seven Wonders of the Ancient World, were supposedly created by Nebuchadnezzar in around 570BCE for his Persian wife, who missed the fertile hills and valleys of her homeland. No trace exists, but later artistic impressions envisage astonishing feats of water engineering – rather like the Duchess of Northumberland's late twentieth-century water garden at Alnwick. Archaeological evidence actually exists of elaborate gardens around Baghdad, dating from the eighth century CE.

Cyrus the Great of Persia (600–530BCE) was said to have had a 'Paradise Garden' – a rectangular space divided into quarters and watered by rills (small ornamental canals). The gardens became more elaborate where there was more water, influencing the Moghul gardens of India, and setting the pattern for gardens visible today in Iran, constructed over the past five centuries or more.

Farming with the Pharaohs

Early inhabitants of the Nile Delta pursued some sort of gardening, using the rich alluvial soil for a range of crops. Cultivated vines are painted on the walls of what nineteenth-century travellers called the Tomb of the Vineyards, which belonged to Sennefer, mayor of Thebes during the reign of Amenhotep II (1439–1413BCE). Even earlier wall engravings hint that the gardens of the affluent were lined with trees, and had lotus ponds framed with acacias and palms.

All Greek to me

The ancient Greeks appear to have had little interest in domestic gardening, although they put gardens around temples. They also produced the first recorded botanist, Theophrastus, who lectured at the Lyceum in around 320BCE. He named some 500 plant species, about half of which appear in Greek poetry; Homer, for instance, mentions sixty.

What have the Romans ever done for us?

When Julius Caesar invaded Britain in 54BCE, he and his followers introduced the Roman love of gardening, as can be seen from the excavated villas at Fishbourne in Sussex and Chedworth in Gloucestershire.

The Romans used a variety of plants medicinally and garlanded their heroes with laurel and palm branches. Wealthy Romans created large, imposing gardens which had waterworks, topiary, arcades and rose gardens. Pliny the Younger wrote about shaded paths with hedges, ornamental parterres (flowerbeds laid out geometrically), fountains, trees and bushes. Three large frescoes, saved from the lava which engulfed Pompeii when Vesuvius erupted in 79CE, depict in accurate and loving detail a luxuriant garden, with lilies, daisies, roses, marigolds, reeds and poppies, through which dance magpies, swallows, a nightingale and a sparrow.

In the Orient

Chinese and Japanese gardens traditionally evoked the natural landscape. The formality of Japanese garden design today, with its green pavilions, use of water and areas of swept gravel, nevertheless still hints at mountain springs, rocky landscapes and the world beyond the garden. This has been the style from time immemorial, while Chinese gardening was influenced for many centuries by the teachings of Confucius (550–479BCE). Gardening was orderly and also had political implications, as Sir William Chambers recognised when comparing British gardening unfavourably with Chinese in the late eighteenth century. 'With the Chinese,' he wrote, 'the taste of Ornamental Gardening is an object of legislative attention; it being supposed to have an influence on the general culture, and consequently upon the beauty of the whole country.'

Garden Fact

In the fourth century CE, the Chinese civil servant and poet Ton Guen-Ming is believed to have dreamt up the penjing, or tray garden, a precursor of bonsai. Bonsai, now thought of as characteristically Japanese, was taken from China to Japan by Buddhist monks in 1195CE.

Keeping the grass green

The sack of Rome by the Visigoths in 410CE ushered in what used to be known as the Dark Ages, now more politely termed Late Antiquity and the early Middle Ages. Eighty years earlier, on his conversion to Christianity, Constantine the Great had founded the Eastern Roman or Byzantine Empire with Constantinople as its capital. This empire lasted until the fall of Constantinople to the Ottomans in 1453. In those eleven centuries, the Byzantines kept the flame of classical civilisation alive, assisted by increasing contact with the Islamic nations of the Middle East and around the Mediterranean from the ninth century onwards. Well-to-do Byzantines initially built large pleasure gardens (*Locus amoenus*), but, as the empire came under threat and the cities shrank, gardens once again became places of retreat (*Hortus conclusus*). The enclosed garden was an earth-bound symbol of heavenly paradise, while the walk around the cloister of a monastery symbolised the path through life.

How fair is a garden amid the trials and passions of existence.
BENJAMIN DISRAELI (1804–1881)

Monks created kitchen gardens, medicinal herb gardens, orchards and vineyards, and stopped mill streams to make fish ponds. Think of Ellis Peters' Brother Cadfael, a canny old monk whose wisdom is derived from contemplating his herb garden – and his knowledge of herbs and spices from his years as a Crusading soldier in the Middle East.

An Italian herbal (or plant directory) published in about 1260 gives instructions for planting grass plots, the first mention of something resembling a lawn. Forty years later, a Bolognese textbook on gardening and agriculture describes gardens surrounded with stone walls, thick hedging or fencing, incorporating trellises and arbours. Their form was borrowed from the rectangular shape of the cloister and included square planting beds.

Meanwhile, the Moors in Spain built palaces and gardens which were both complex and sophisticated. The Alhambra in Granada, for instance, developed from a ninth-century hill fortress. The surrounding gardens and those of the adjacent Generalife, still some of the finest in the world, date from the fourteenth century.

Renaissance in gardening

Gardens in Renaissance Europe harked back to the glory that was Rome. Full of stone statues of gods and goddesses evoking scenes from ancient mythology and with topiary, terracing, sacred groves, secret gardens and extravagant waterworks, gardens were designed for the leaders of the city states to display their power and taste. Gardening was also developing as a scientific study: the first European botanic garden was founded in Pisa in 1544, followed the next year by one in Padua, and, in 1550, by one in Florence.

English pastoral

Herbals were already big business in Tudor England. The first illustrated English herbal, *The Grete Herbal*, was published in London in 1526, to be followed in 1538 by William Turner's *Libellus de re Herbaria novus*, in which he took 144 plants and gave their synonyms in Greek and English (Turner was an admirer of Theophrastus).

The pastoral was by now firmly embedded in English poetry. It runs through Edmund Spenser's *Faerie Queene* (1590) and through the works of Shakespeare. His detailed plant descriptions reflect his Warwickshire childhood and show that the playwright was as observant of ordinary gardens as he was of people. The English were clearly already a keen gardening nation, able to appreciate his allusions.

Age of exploration

Gardens were for show in England, too. On Elizabeth I's death, her chief minister Robert Cecil seamlessly transferred his allegiance to her Stuart successor, James I. His garden at Theobalds in Hertfordshire, with canal, maze, white marble fountains and glittering array of plants, was so magnificent that the king persuaded Cecil to swap Theobalds for the old royal palace of Hatfield. There, Cecil employed John Tradescant the Elder, an early British plant hunter, who travelled to Russia, France, the Low Countries and North Africa.

With the discovery of the Americas, and the growth of travel, plant hunting intensified. Sir Walter Raleigh famously introduced tobacco to Britain, while John Tradescant the Younger travelled to Barbados and Virginia, bringing back Virginia creeper, the tulip tree, Michaelmas daisies and the eponymous *Tradescantia virginiana*.

New plants from the eastern Mediterranean and Turkey (the tulip came to Europe from there in the 1570s) became widely available. In courtly and noble gardens, intricate beds of planting were outlined by hedges and topiary shapes of yew and bay, owing much in style to the Persian paradise gardens. In country gardens, flowers grew through vegetables and fruit trees scrambled up walls.

The absolute garden

As garden statements go, few can be more show-stopping than Le Nôtre's great work for Louis XIV at Versailles. Its rigid formalism, vast fountains, groves of statuary, and invocation of Apollo as an image for the Sun King, make this garden the ultimate expression of absolutism, and the divinity of the monarch.

Meanwhile in England, Louis's first cousin, James II, was deposed by a nation suspicious of both Catholicism and absolutism, and replaced by his daughter, Mary, and her Dutch husband, William of Orange. William introduced the water garden from his own garden at Het Loo, with canals lined by clipped topiary. The English toyed briefly with the style: the only surviving example is at Westbury Court by the Severn in Gloucestershire.

He leaped the fence

> *All gardening is landscape painting.*
> WILLIAM KENT (1685–1748)

The English landscape movement dominated eighteenth-century gardening. The terraces, walls and fancy topiary of Stuart and French-style gardens were swept away and replaced by a much more naturalistic approach, the main exponents of which were Charles Bridgeman, William Kent and Lancelot 'Capability' Brown. Bridgeman removed topiary and parterres, and planted wide avenues, while Kent, who, in Horace Walpole's famous phrase, 'leaped the fence and saw all nature was a garden', softened the landscape. Trees followed natural contours, and water tripped down over stones rather than being forced up into the air by fountains. Later in the century, Brown turned landscape gardens into open parkland, with grazing sheep and deer, kept from approaching the house by a ha-ha.

Ha-ha

The ha-ha was probably of French origin (although Walpole credited Bridgeman with its invention), and was so called because, in Walpole's words, the ditch was 'so astonishing, that the common people called them Ha! Has! to express their surprise at finding a sudden and unperceived check to their walk'.

Looking west

At the end of the eighteenth century, the founding fathers of the new American republic made gardens for their pleasure and delight, and also with political intent. Washington, Jefferson, Adams and Madison used native plants, yet, despite their familiarity with European gardens, avoided copying them. Washington, returning home to Mount Vernon, redesigned his garden, releasing it from its geometric corset as he had freed his nation from British tyranny. Madison, an early environmentalist, sought to restore the balance of nature on his estate at Montpelier.

The Kew effect

In 1759, George III's mother, Augusta, Dowager Princess of Wales, founded Kew Gardens, unusually combining a botanic with a landscape garden. That *annus mirabilis* saw the effective defeat of France and the emergence of Britain as a world power, with consequences for the nation's gardens. In the 1770s, Sir Joseph Banks, as director of Kew Gardens, began sending out plant hunters around the empire to face considerable dangers, and even death, in the search for new botanical specimens.

High Victorianism

Gardening became a much more general pursuit in the Victorian age, with the growing middle class, under instruction from J. C. Loudon, making gardens with lawns and neat flowerbeds behind suburban villas. Allotments had already become important both for urban gardeners and for needy country people by the late eighteenth century, with some factory owners providing plots of land for their workers.

For the wealthy, it was the age of the grand conservatory (thanks to the development of glazing bars), and the 200-foot dahlia border, of pinetums and arboretums. All were labour-intensive and lavish forms of gardening, as was the equally popular carpet bedding – elaborately patterned schemes which involved replanting annuals and bulbs twice a year or more.

The invention of the lawnmower in 1830 eventually paved the way – to mix metaphors – for the more general use of grass in gardens across the country.

Flowers and trees

In 1883 William Robinson published *The English Flower Garden*, in which he attacked the formal bedding schemes so beloved of the Victorians. Robinson influenced Gertrude Jekyll, who, like him, favoured the flowing, more naturalistic effect of herbaceous perennials, rather than stylised beds of annuals. She planted in the Arts and Crafts style of the time, within a firm stone framework provided by her partner, Edwin Lutyens.

Landowners sponsored plant-hunters such as Edward Wilson, George Forrest, Frank Kingdon-Ward and Reginald Farrer, who gathered plants across the Far East, introducing rhododendrons, roses and rock plants, which became accepted features of the British garden. Rock gardens, in particular, were the rage through the first half of the twentieth century.

Après le déluge

Legions of gardeners who left to fight in the First World War never returned. Many grand kitchen gardens and greenhouses fell into dereliction, with a few, such as Aberglasney and Heligan, being rediscovered almost a century later. Woodland plants became fashionable, but on the whole even large gardens, such as Hidcote and Sissinghurst, were planted on a smaller scale, with separate 'rooms', each having its own ethos. These two influential gardens introduced a romantic, perennial style of planting, with a strong seasonal emphasis.

The mid-war suburban garden featured a small lawn, flanked by beds of standard roses surrounded by bare earth. There might also be a vegetable garden and serried rows of dahlias or chrysanthemums, grown to garner cups at the local flower shows which became popular in the 1920s and 1930s.

The Second World War changed gardens again, as people were urged to dig for victory and plough up their lawns for vegetables. In the post-war years, many gardeners continued to grow vegetables, often on allotments, and the taste for annuals gave a gaudy formality to gardens of the fifties and sixties.

High society

Growing interest in gardening and in individual plants can be seen from the formation of specialist societies in the nineteenth and twentieth centuries. These are a few significant societies:

Royal Horticultural Society	*1804*
Royal National Rose Society	*1876*
Daffodil Society	*1898*
British Iris Society	*1922*
British Gladiolus Society	*1926*
Delphinium Society	*1928*
Alpine Garden Society	*1929*
Hardy Plant Society	*1957*

Gardening now

Despite increasing mechanisation in many areas of life, gardeners still use the tools of their forebears. We may have programmed irrigation and garden lighting, sit-upon or robotic mowers and electric hedge trimmers, but most of the donkey work is still done with shears and secateurs, and a spade, fork and trowel. Gardening styles reflect this, as gardeners continue to like the connection with the soil.

Important late twentieth-century figures include Beth Chatto, who started her Essex garden in 1960. Swimming against the current of the time, she emphasised the importance of choosing plants for places where they will flourish, rather than shoe-horning them into pre-ordained schemes. Hardy perennials gradually began to become as popular as annual plants, while a flurry of ladylike romanticism was reintroduced by gardeners such as Rosemary Verey and Alvide Lees-Milne, who filled their gardens with flowers and scent.

In the last decade of the twentieth century, a new wind blew in from across the North Sea bringing the 'New Perennial' movement. The Dutch garden designer, Piet Oudolf, advocated the planting of perennials in bold drifts, interspersed by bands of grasses, all chosen for their shape and texture as much as for their colour. The British garden designer Tom Stuart-Smith has adapted this style and made it his own, sprinkling jewel-like flowers through geometric blocks of green and whispering grasses.

The natural development from Beth Chatto's 'right plant in the right place' philosophy has been ecological and wildlife gardens, spurred on by concerns about climate change and epitomised by the London Olympics gardens designed by James Hitchmough, Nigel Dunnett and Sarah Price. The emphasis in the gardens was on sustainability and low maintenance, with perennials mixed with grasses through meadows, wetlands and parkland. Key plants included fashionable umbellifers, rudbeckias, echinacea, kniphofia, and stands of acers and birches.

Royal progress

If you want to get a flavour of the variety of styles currently enjoying popularity, then club together with twenty-three friends and book a visit to the Prince of Wales's garden at Highgrove in Gloucestershire. In this highly personal, if not to say idiosyncratic garden, you will see a modern take on a parterre and allée (steered by Rosemary Verey and Roy Strong), a clipped box garden, a stumpery (the work of Isabel and Julian Bannerman), a contemporary hermitage, a wildlife meadow and a productive potager.

Now and then

In the early twenty-first century, the wheel has come full-circle, with enterprising gardener-cooks now going out, as their pre-historic ancestors did 10,000 years ago, to forage. Visit any chic little bistro in a provincial town and you may be presented with a pannacotta made from sea buckthorn gathered from along the seashore or a bay bolete (mushroom) omelette unearthed in local woodland. The ancients probably didn't make pannacottas, but otherwise, *plus ça change, plus c'est la même chose*.

10,000BCE	Mankind begins enclosing land to make primitive settlements
3,000BCE	Sumerian tribes irrigate the land between the Tigris and the Euphrates
1,600BCE	Egyptian wall paintings hint at ornamental horticulture and elementary landscape design
570BCE	Creation of the mythical Hanging Gardens of Babylon
320BCE	Theophrastus teaches at the Lyceum in Athens and identifies differences and similarities between plants
61BCE	Pliny the Younger describes geometric Roman gardens with fountains and lavish planting
54BCE	Julius Caesar invades Britain
79CE	Destruction of Pompeii. Recovered wall paintings reveal detailed knowledge of plants and planting
300CE	Chinese invention of penjing, precursor of bonsai
330CE	Foundation of the Eastern Roman (Byzantine) Empire by Constantine (lasts until 1453). Over the next millennium, the Byzantine Empire and the Arab peoples of the Middle East and Mediterranean keep formal gardening traditions alive
700CE	Archaeological evidence of elaborate gardens around Baghdad
995CE	Abbot Aelfric's Glossary to *Grammatica Latino-Saxonica* lists 200 British plants
1100 onwards	Age of the monastic garden in Europe, with gardens invested with religious and spiritual significance

1195	Bonsai introduced to Japan from China by Buddhist monks
1260	Garden grass first mentioned in Albertus Magnus's *De Vegetabilibus*
1300s	Creation of the gardens of the Generalife and the Alhambra in Granada, Spain
1455–61	Italian Renaissance garden created at the Villa Medici, Fiesole, near Florence
1526	Publication of *The Grete Herbal*, the first illustrated English herbal
1536–1540	Dissolution of the Monasteries and the destruction of monastic gardens in England and Wales
1544	First European botanic garden opens in Pisa
1550–1572	High Renaissance garden created at Villa d'Este, Tivoli, Rome
1570	Introduction of the tulip to Europe from Turkey by the Imperial ambassador Ogier Ghiselin de Busbecq
1597	Publication of John Gerard's *Herball*
1618	John Tradescant the Elder travels with a diplomatic mission to Russia, introducing angelica and the Muscovy briar to England
1621	Establishment of England's first botanic garden at the University of Oxford
1630s	John Tradescant the Younger plant hunts in Virginia and Barbados

1673	Creation of the Chelsea Physic Garden
1689–1702	During his reign, William of Orange redesigned the gardens at Hampton Court and inspired a short-lived fashion for canal gardens
1713–1760	The English Landscape movement
1759	The foundation of Kew Gardens by Augusta, Dowager Princess of Wales
1760–1820	The Picturesque movement and the birth of British tourism in the Wye Valley
1770s	A wave of plant hunting around the globe is initiated by Sir Joseph Banks
1776	The American Declaration of Independence. Over the next half century, the first presidents create significant gardens and estates
1804	The foundation of the Royal Horticultural Society by Sir Joseph Banks and John Wedgwood in Hatchards bookshop in Piccadilly, London
1837–1901	Queen Victoria's reign, during which a taste for Italianate gardens was reborn (led by her work at Osborne House on the Isle of Wight) and the fashion for conservatories and carpet bedding reached its height
1883	William Robinson publishes *The English Flower Garden*
1890s–1920s	The age of the plant-hunters, including E. H. Wilson, George Forrest, Reginald Farrah and Frank Kingdon-Ward
1900–1914	Key years of the influential gardening partnership of Gertrude Jekyll and Sir Edwin Lutyens
1907–1947	The creation of Hidcote in Gloucestershire by Lawrence Johnston

1913	The first Chelsea Flower Show
1914–1918	The First World War helps to bring about the end of the great estate gardens
1929–1962	The creation of Sissinghurst Castle garden in Kent by Vita Sackville-West and Harold Nicolson
1939–1945	The Second World War encourages people to 'Dig for Victory', and to turn flower gardens into vegetable gardens
1950s	Margery Fry recreates the cottage garden style at East Lambrook Manor in Somerset
1960	Beth Chatto starts work on her garden near Colchester in Essex
1970s	Rosemary Verey creates her ornamental potager at Barnsley House in Gloucestershire
1980s	The Prince of Wales begins work on his garden at Highgrove in Gloucestershire
Late 1990s	Piet Oudolf introduces the New Perennial movement into Britain from the Netherlands
1997	The Duchess of Northumberland begins work on the Alnwick water garden
2013	The Chelsea Flower Show celebrates its centenary

Some major Garden Moments

- The fall of man in the Garden of Eden – which is where it all began

- The arrest of Jesus Christ among the olive groves of the Garden of Gethsemane

- 1455 – The plucking of the red and white roses in the Temple Garden, triggering the Wars of the Roses (apocryphal, of course, and based on a scene in Shakespeare's *Henry VI, Part I*)

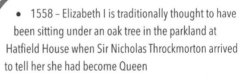

- 1558 – Elizabeth I is traditionally thought to have been sitting under an oak tree in the parkland at Hatfield House when Sir Nicholas Throckmorton arrived to tell her she had become Queen

- 1651 – After his defeat at the Battle of Worcester, Charles II hid from the Parliamentary forces in an oak tree in the garden of Boscobel House in Shropshire

- 1680s – Watching an apple fall from a tree in the garden of Trinity College, Cambridge, allegedly inspired Sir Isaac Newton's theory of gravity (descendants of the apple tree still stand in Trinity's garden, in the University of Cambridge Botanic Garden and in the garden of the Instituto Balseiro library in Argentina)

- 1788 – What is it about oak trees? In the shade of an oak tree at Holwood House near Hayes, William Wilberforce announced to William Pitt the Younger that he intended to bring an end to the slave trade (a third replacement oak now grows on the site)

- 1992 – The photographs of Diana, Princess of Wales, sitting alone in the gardens of the Taj Mahal signalled the collapse of her marriage to Prince Charles

CHAPTER 2

GARDENING ALLSORTS

Consult the genius of the place in all.
ALEXANDER POPE (1688–1744)

Don't believe those gardening makeover programmes: there is no such thing as a maintenance-free garden. You can redesign a room, and your new look will stay put. Not so with gardens. When Piet Oudolf designed the new double borders at the Royal Horticultural Society's Wisley garden, he told the gardeners that they would probably have to replant up to twenty per cent within two years because the plants wouldn't have behaved as he had anticipated.

For the rest of us: turn your back for a weekend and you'll find the grass wants cutting, the roses deadheading, and the slugs and snails have launched a concerted attack on the rudbeckias. But before I put you off the idea of gardening entirely, remember that the whole point of gardening is to garden. Suggesting that a gardener might not want to garden is like suggesting that a runner might like to complete a marathon without running.

There are as many gardening styles as there are gardeners, and tastes change as they do in the world of fashion. Finding the right look for your garden depends on many factors, including the age of your property, its location, soil and aspect. But, to get the hoe hoeing, here is a far from exhaustive list of some of the styles you might like to consider.

The cottage garden

This quintessential English favourite is the look that always wins the people's vote at Chelsea and which is encapsulated by this description: 'A magnificent country cottage in the English style, overgrown with masses of fragrant flowers, with flower-beds all round it; a porch, wreathed with climbing plants and surrounded by beds of roses'. This, you may imagine, is an account from a late nineteenth-century English gardening book, but no, it's Dostoyevsky's tortured anti-hero, Raskolnikov, for whom such a garden represents a wonderful dream as he faces penal servitude in Siberia. There is a sense of abundance about the cottage garden, with flowers planted in billowing borders, and mixed with vegetables and fruit. It overlaps with the Arts and Crafts garden of the late nineteenth century, in that both use local, natural materials, although an Arts and Crafts garden tends to be more formal in layout with stone or low box bushes edging the beds. For a real cottage feel, let *Alchemilla mollis* flop onto your lawn or paths, pack your beds with plants such as poppies, hardy geraniums, daisies, roses, nepeta and lavender, and plant a couple of small apple or pear trees.

The kitchen garden

The kitchen garden has a long history, its roots lying in medieval monasteries. A century ago, all great estates would have had a productive walled kitchen garden, mostly situated at some distance from the house. South-facing walls would have been espaliered with fruit trees, and there might also have been an orchard, with apples, pears and cherry trees. The gardens would have been laid out in a formal pattern, with wigwams of sweet peas and beans, and vegetables planted rotationally through the seasons (potatoes being the first planting to break up the soil). A bed would have been reserved for cut flowers for the house. In the 1970s, Rosemary Verey created an ornamental potager, based in part on seventeenth-century pattern books, which reignited an interest in mixing flowers and vegetables but in an orderly, symmetrical fashion. If you only have a balcony, you can still have a kitchen garden, by growing lettuces, sweetcorn, tomatoes, herbs and various fruits in pots. Elsewhere, raised beds will save your back, and, if you don't have a wall for espaliers, then consider lining your paths with step-over apples.

The wildlife garden

Wildlife gardening became increasingly popular in the late twentieth/early twenty-first century. Our gardening ancestors knew quite well how to maintain the balance in nature, but we somehow lost the plot around the Second World War and starting blitzing our gardens with chemicals. I used to spray all the time and found blackfly a scourge. Now, I let well alone and the garden is abuzz with other insects who do the job for me. What wildlife gardening entails is making a haven for birds, hedgehogs, bees, butterflies and ladybirds who, between them, will take care of most of your garden pests. You need to grow a wide range of nectar plants throughout the spring and summer (winter honeysuckle, foxgloves, buddleia and *Verbena bonariensis* are all great for bees and butterflies). You can't be too kempt, either, as piles of logs and leaves and areas of long grass should be left as comfortable habitats for hedgehogs, bees, ladybirds and small birds.

The sensory garden

In the twenty-first century, there has been a determined drive to make gardens accessible to those with disabilities. Chelsea designer Cleve West created a memorial garden at a spinal unit in Salisbury in 2012, where he built wide, smooth paths and raised beds, and focused on scent, taste, texture and colour in his planting. Use scented plants such as herbs, roses and lavender for summer, and winter-flowering honeysuckle, *Lonicera fragrantissima*, and sarcococca for winter, which can be enjoyed by the sighted and non-sighted alike. Soft-leafed rabbit's ears (*Stachys byzantina*) gives a tactile edging to a border, while the breeze will whisper through grasses such as Stipa, panicum and Miscanthus.

The allotment

Allotments are, in effect, the continuation of the feudal strip-farm system, in which every peasant had a parcel of land to work (many of which disappeared with enclosures). Well established around towns, factories and villages by the late eighteenth century, allotments enjoyed a particular heyday after the Second World War. Often allocated unwanted land, they were, nevertheless, useful places on which to produce extra food when rationing was still in place. Allotment gardening has enjoyed a revival since the late 1990s, with the new emphasis on cutting food miles, growing your own, and community activity. An allotment will distract you from your own garden, but it will be worth it for the flavour of your own fresh potatoes, greens, beans and lettuces. You may need to be patient, though; you can expect to wait for years for an allotment in some inner-city areas.

The seaside garden

If you live by the sea, you will, de facto, have a seaside garden, and you'll have to garden accordingly. The variety of looks are dictated by the garden's location. Sheltered, lush Devon valleys, warmed by the Gulf Stream, are very different from the drier, windswept gardens of East Anglia. On the beach at Dungeness, the film director Derek Jarman created a garden in touch with the raw side of nature, with shards of flint poking up through shingle, and seathrift and seakale dotted around as they would be on a clifftop walk. West or east, you'll need planting that's resistant to strong winds and seaspray, including spiky phormiums, fuchsia and escallonia, with privet, perhaps, as a wind break. On the west coast, you'll be able to grow tree ferns, camellias, magnolias and hydrangeas, and probably even over-winter cannas and ginger lilies. On the east coast, go for sea buckthorn, thrift and *Crambe maritima*.

The rock garden

For the first half of the twentieth century, rock gardening was all the rage. This owed much to the eccentric and single-minded plant hunter Reginald Farrah who travelled extensively in the mountains of China and Tibet in the first two decades of the twentieth century. The range of new plants he sent back to the UK, including primulas and gentians, helped to put a rockery in every British back garden. Long out of fashion, rock gardening is perhaps due a revival, as it's ideal for gardeners struggling with a limey soil. Campanulas, larkspur, violas, saxifrages, small sedums and houseleeks will all thrive in rockeries, which have the added advantage that they can be created in miniature or in old sinks in small gardens, and placed at eye level so you can enjoy every detail.

The New Perennial garden

Piet Oudolf's New Perennial look was an exciting gardening development in the late twentieth century. The Dutch garden designer and nurseryman built on the increasing popularity of herbaceous planting, but took it in a radical new direction. His style involves planting bold drifts of perennials and grasses, chosen as much for their structure and foliage shape and texture as for their flowers. His naturalised planting gives a long season of interest, and the seedheads are a magnet to bees and other insects. You could try a watered-down version in a small town garden by buying substantial quantities of a few plants and growing them in clumps, interspersed with grasses.

The lawn garden

This is one for the lads, really. Ask any couple how they divide their gardening chores, and you'll find the woman tends the flowerbeds, and the chap chops everything down and mows the lawn. When I was a child, our neighbours always knew we were back from our holiday when they heard the roar of my father's motor mower. It's the image of Sunday in suburbia: the men up and down with their mowers, creating those sleek alternate lines of green and razor-sharp edges. But there's more to lawn-making than mowing; you also need to water, feed, control the weeds and moss, scarify, aerate and top-dress to get that immaculate smooth green look. Maybe that's one of the reasons why lawns are in retreat, along with a current desire for a more relaxed look, with flowers spilling out from their beds. You might want to consider other alternatives, such as chamomile or thyme. And, if you are prepared for your lawn to look like a school tennis court, the ultimate in labour-saving lawns has to be one of fake grass, which only needs the occasional sweep.

The Mediterranean garden

The British have a long-standing love affair with the Mediterranean, enjoying the aromatic scent of its vegetation on a sunny day or on the evening air. Add that to periods of drought and hose-pipe bans, and you can see why Mediterranean-style gardening has become popular in recent years. It also has the advantage of being relatively maintenance-light once you've planted it up and laid down the gravel (over a weed-proof membrane). Run the fragrant and prolific climber, *Trachelospermum jasminoides*, up a south-facing wall, and choose trees such as figs, bays, laurel and olives (the latter best planted in frost-resistant pots) to give the garden structure. Typical Mediterranean planting includes lavender, grown in sinuous lines through the gravel, verbascums, euphorbia, yucca, and sage, rosemary and thyme. Compact agapanthus in tight pots to encourage them to flower profusely.

The Japanese garden

Japanese gardening style depends on the precision and attention to detail shown in recent Gold medal-winning gardens by the inimitable Ishihara Kazuyuki at the Chelsea Flower Show. Key elements include water, trickling down over tiny rocky cascades (which can be fitted into a corner and operated by an electric pump); fine, frequently swept gravel as a background to planting; and architectural, shaped trees. Multi-stemmed, specimen birches, acers or pines will give the garden structure, together with cloud-pruned hollies, box or yew. Low-level planting should include mosses and ferns (ideal for town gardens with little sunlight), with water irises in pools for contrast. Bamboo can be used as a screen against neighbours or the unsightly working parts of the garden.

The clipped garden

I use the word 'clipped' to denote shear-control, including knot gardens, topiary and turf mazes. For those who like order, shape and year-round interest in their gardens, then clipping is the thing. There's a splendid choice of suitable evergreens, including yew, bay, holly, myrtle and phillyrea. It's an ancient tradition: the Romans packed their gardens with box hedging and topiary. Knot gardens were particularly popular with the Tudors and Stuarts, although they used lavender, bay or holly for their miniature hedges, disliking the smell of box. A knot garden, filled with gravel, or planted with bulbs for spring and annuals for summer, makes a pleasing front garden if you don't need hard-standing for your car, while topiaried roundels, pyramids and columns give structure and winter shape. And, if you want to add humour, buy wire frames shaped like cats or chickens, and clip your evergreen around them.

How to start a garden, or ten things you need...

1. Patience – despite what all those TV makeover programmes suggest, gardens take time to mature and develop

2. A cast-iron back

3. To get a sense of the garden's character by looking at the surrounding buildings and landscape

4. To wait a year to see what comes up before you start planting anything new

5. To assess what seems to be flourishing in nearby gardens and grow similar types of plants

6. To know your soil, which you can test with a little pH kit, bought from any garden centre. You can improve it over time, but it's not worth trying to grow the wrong plant in the wrong soil.

7. To track the path of the sun and remember that in winter, the low sun may leave large areas in the shade all day

8. To see whether you can borrow views from other gardens or the countryside beyond, or whether you want to enclose your own green oasis

9. To check your boundaries and the existing hard materials before you start pulling down fences and digging up paths

10. Oh, and did I mention patience? That's needed in spades

Where to see different garden styles

The cottage garden

- RHS Garden Wisley, Woking GU23 6QB (0845 260 9000; www.rhs.org.uk/gardens/wisley)
- Sissinghurst Castle, Cranbrook, Kent TN17 2AB (01580 710700; www.nationaltrust.org.uk/sissinghurst-castle)

The kitchen garden

- Rosemary Verey's Potager, Barnsley House, Cirencester, Gloucestershire GL7 5EE (01285 740000; www.barnsleyhouse.com). By appointment
- Villandry Castle & Gardens, 37510 Villandry, France (0 33 [0] 2 47 50 02 09; www.chateauvillandry.fr)

The wildlife garden

- Fairhaven Woodland & Water Garden, South Walsham, Norfolk NR13 6DZ (01603 270449; www.fairhavengarden.co.uk)
- Natural History Museum, London SW7 5BD (020 7942 5000; www.nhm.ac.uk)

The sensory garden

- Chatsworth, Bakewell, Derbyshire DE45 1PP (01246 565300; www.chatsworth.org)
- Polesworth Abbey, near Tamworth, Warwickshire B78 1DU (01827 892340; www.polesworthabbey.heralded.org.uk)

The allotment

- Chiswick House Kitchen Garden, London W4 2RP (020 8742 3905; www.chgt.org.uk)
- The National Allotment Society (01536 266576; www.nsalg.org.uk)

The seaside garden

- Derek Jarman's garden, Prospect Cottage. Visible from the private road to the National Nature Reserve at Dungeness, Kent (Romney Marsh Countryside Project, 01797 367934; www.rmcp.co.uk)
- Overbeck's, Salcombe, Devon TQ8 8LW (01548 842893; www.nationaltrust.org.uk/overbecks)

The rock garden

- The Beth Chatto Gardens, Elmstead Market, Essex CO7 7DB (01206 822007; www.bethchatto.co.uk)
- Royal Botanic Gardens, Kew, Richmond, Surrey TW9 3AB (020 8332 5655; www.kew.org)

The New Perennial garden

- Millennium Garden, Pensthorpe, Fakenham, Norfolk NR21 0LN (01328 851465; www.pensthorpe.com)
- The Walled Garden, Scampston Estate, Malton, North Yorkshire YO17 8NG (01944 759111; www.scampston.co.uk)

The lawn garden

- The Courts Garden, Bradford-upon-Avon, Somerset BA14 6RR (01225 782875; www.nationaltrust.org.uk/courts-garden)
- Dyffryn Gardens, St Nicholas, Glamorgan CF5 6SU (0290 593328; www.nationaltrust.org.uk/dyffryn-gardens)

The Mediterranean garden

- Mount Stewart, Newtownards, County Down BT22 2AD (028 4278 8387; www.nationaltrust.org.uk/mount-stewart)
- Tresco Abbey, Isles of Scilly TR24 0PU (01720 424105; www.tresco.co.uk/what-to-do/abbey-garden/)

The Japanese garden

- 'Pure Land' Japanese Garden, North Clifton, Nottinghamshire NG23 7AT (01777 228567; www.buddhamaitreya.co.uk)
- Tatton Park, Knutsford, Cheshire WA16 6QN (01625 374435; www.nationaltrust.org.uk/tatton-park)

The clipped garden

- Packwood House, Lapworth, Warwickshire B94 6AT (01564 782024; www.nationaltrust.org.uk/packwood-house)
- Levens Hall, Kendal, Cumbria LA8 0PD (01539 560321; www.levenshall.co.uk)

CHAPTER 3

GARDENING PARAPHERNALIA, OR GETTING DOWN TO IT

What a man needs in gardening is a cast-iron back, with a hinge in it.
CHARLES DUDLEY WARNER (1829–1900)

Look in any garden shed today and you'll see tools which could have been used by our ancestors thousands of years ago. Even if they are now made from different materials, you'll probably find a spade, a hoe, a dibber and some kind of sharp knife or billhook beside the motor mower and the electric hedge trimmer. For the basic gardening tasks remain unchanged: digging, planting, pruning and harvesting.

Preparing the soil

The first tools were probably made from animal bones in about 10,000BCE, just when man was beginning to enclose land and sow a few crops. He needed to turn over the soil, so it is thought that mattocks (or picks) were constructed from sheep's horns lashed to sticks, and shovels from the shoulder blades of oxen. Diggers (or dibbers) are also one of the most ancient of garden tools, originally long sticks with a sharpened end, made from stone or animal ribs, and used to dig a hole to plant seeds or bulbs.

The remains of the iron parts of hoes, forks and rakes were found at Pompeii, while spades were relatively common in Roman Britain, although were probably short-handled and back-breaking to use. Long-handled spades came later, and certainly by the 1170s, as can be seen from a stained-glass window at Canterbury Cathedral dating from then. This shows Adam standing upright and digging with a long-handled spade. His tool has an open D handle, but eventually the T-bar handle became more popular as it gives greater leverage.

Planting

The first known use of a trowel (from the Latin 'trulla' or ladle) was in the thirteenth century and it was subsequently listed in a 1389 inventory for Abingdon Abbey. The trowel, according to Samuel Orchart Beeton, in *The Beeton Book of Garden Management* (1861), is 'a tool that no-one can possibly do without… in planting and transplanting and in potting'.

It's fair enough to scoop up enough earth to plant a few seedlings, but it's a different matter when it comes to bulbs. Which is why some bright spark came up with the idea of a tool with a circular drum, expanding sides and a sharp bottom edge. The sides open out to lift up a wedge of soil and provide a neat hole for the bulb. When the sides of the drum are depressed, the soil slips back down. It appears like a handle-less tin in Giovanni Baptista Ferrari's *Flora* from 1633, although today's bulb planters commonly have retractable D-shaped handles.

Garden handbooks proliferated in the sixteenth and seventeenth centuries. For Thomas Tusser, writing *Five Hundred Points of Good Husbandrie* in 1573, the essential tools for laying out a garden were 'dibble, rake, mattock, and spade… line… and levell'. The latter two were needed to ensure that beds were laid out in the strictly geometric fashion of the day.

Rakes… This tool, is in the Gardener's Trade, a symbol of Neatness.
FRANCIS GENTIL, *LE JARDINIER SOLITAIRE* (1706)

Ho-hoe and more

Hoes predate the plough, and were used then, as now, to turn over the soil and to keep weeds at bay. Its original invention was attributed to Enlil, the chief of the council of gods in Sumerian mythology. The hand-plough (another back-breaking tool) was depicted in Egyptian wall paintings and mentioned in the Book of Isaiah. The modern spelling of the word dates from the eighteenth century.

There are two main classes of hoe, of which the earliest version was the draw hoe. The other, the Dutch thrust or scuffle hoe, has never been as popular in the British Isles.

Until the nineteenth century, the variety in hoe design was legion, with blades which were triangular, rectangular, swan-necked, crick-necked or spurred. Post-industrialisation mass-production led to greater uniformity.

By the time of the Pharaohs, a very basic cultivator, drawn by mules or oxen, had also been added to the gardener's armoury of hoes and mattocks, judging by wall paintings. Leap forward thousands of years and we find the powered rotary hoe being devised in 1912 by Arthur Clifford Howard on his father's farm in Australia. These rotary tillers soon gained popularity with vegetable gardeners in particular who needed to turn the soil over several times before planting their crops. His palindromic Rotavator was patented by Howard in the 1930s. It was equipped with a gearbox and driven forward, or held back by its wheels.

> *The common character of tools is that they are adapted for labour which requires more force than skill. They are generally large and require the use of both hands and the muscular action of the whole frame, often aided by gravity.*
>
> J. C. LOUDON, *ENCYCLOPAEDIA OF GARDENING* (1822)

Cutting and pruning

The Romans, with their fondness for topiary, would have used scissors and shears. In 1572, Leonard Mascall published *A booke of the arte and maner, howe to plant and graffe all sorts of trees*. This manual featured an illustration of the eleven tools Mascall deemed essential for any gardener, over half of which were cutting implements.

The fruit garden grew in importance in the 1500s, and so, over the next three centuries, the types of knives, slashers, shears and saws multiplied dramatically. Knives and saws for pruning and grafting continued to be the key tools for fruit gardeners until the mid-nineteenth century. Francis Gentil, writing in *Le Jardin Solitaire* in 1706, describes a pruning knife as 'So necessary, that a Gardener ought always to have one in his pocket.'

The seventeenth century saw the invention of tree pruners, while the first patent was taken out for hedge clippers in 1860. Secateurs are probably a nineteenth-century invention, their name coming from the French word for cutters. The strong, central spring design has changed very little in the last fifty or sixty years.

Hedging your bets

In the seventeenth and early eighteenth century, the fashion was for elaborate topiary and mazes, and for clipped hedges. A series of eight paintings of the gardens at Hartwell House in Buckinghamshire by Balthasar Nebot, from about 1738, shows one gardener trimming the hedge with handshears and another picking up the clippings and putting them in a basket.

> *There's a divinity that shapes our ends,*
> *Rough-hew them how we will.*
> WILLIAM SHAKESPEARE, *HAMLET, V.II* (1600)

The first mechanised hedge trimmer was conceived in Idaho in 1854. It had geared wheels, a nearly vertical cutting wheel and side to side cutters, and was horse-drawn. In 1891 a patent was taken out for a mobile, hand-held cutting device, which was still cumbersome and unwieldy. The Little Wonder Organisation moved things forward in 1922 with the marketing of a hedge trimmer with a handcrank, followed by a hand-held single trimmer (1940), then in 1945 by a double-bladed one. The first petrol-driven hedge cutter appeared in 1955, since when the technology has evolved considerably. Hedge trimmers are now lighter, while expensive modern versions have pivoting grips to cut into difficult angles.

Garden Fact

An estimated 17 million gallons of gasoline are spilled each summer while refuelling garden and lawncare equipment in the United States. That's about 50 per cent more than was spilled during the Exxon Valdez incident.

Mowing

In 1259 the newly laid turf at the Palace of Westminster was rolled with a marble roller. This seems a far cry from today's plastic roller, which is lightweight to transport, and can be filled with water when needed for rolling, then emptied for storage.

Gardeners are seen scything the grass in the 1738 Hartwell sequence of pictures, and scythes continued to be used for cutting lawns until as recently as the 1940s. Getting a successfully even cut was a skilled business, but three experienced mowers could manage an acre of lawn in a day.

By the 1740s, Sheffield mills were manufacturing scythes for mowing, and the first mass-produced riveted scythe of iron and steel was patented in 1791 by Abraham Hill, a Sheffield saw-maker.

Lawn technology moved on as the Victorians made parks and gardens for their villas, even while some gardeners were still scything grass. The first lawnmower was patented by Edwin Budding in 1830, to be followed by a steam-powered lawnmower in 1893, and the first rotary mower in 1933. The rotary-action leaf sweeper and lawn-edgers gave a groomed and sharp finish to a well-cut lawn from the mid-nineteenth century.

In 1962, Flymo AB took out a patent for a mower which hovered over the lawn, and was an immediate success. More recently, robotic mowers have taken the physical labour out of mowing by buzzing across the lawn on their own. The lovers of clear mowing lines may, however, be less than charmed by a robomower's erratic journey.

Watering

In the Middle Ages, monks were already using channels, conduits and lead pipes (an early version of the seepy hose) to move water to their vegetable and herb gardens.

In 1577, writing in his book, *The Gardener's Labyrinth*, Thomas Hill gave the first description of a sprinkler device, in a detailed section called 'The Manner of Watering with a Pumpe in a Tubbe':

> *The vessel… must be set into a deepe vessel or tube of water, in what place of the garden the… Gardener mindeth to begin in drawing first the pump up, and with mightier strength thrusting it downe againe, which so handled, causeth the water to ascend and flee forth of the pipe holes on such height, that in the falling, the droppes come downe through the aire, breaking it in the forme of raine.'*

According to the Oxford English Dictionary, 1580 saw the first appearance of the term 'watering-pot', with 'watering-can' ensuing in 1692. Hoses were originally made of quickly perishable canvas, then of leather. A process for riveting leather was developed in 1811, while in 1827 Thomas Hancock of Fulham conceived the India rubber hose, which had a slightly longer life. It wasn't until the 1950s that the first plastic hose was sold.

Since the first lawn sprinkler was patented in the 1870s, technology has changed relatively little. The major new development has been the invention of expensive automatic watering systems.

Protection from the elements

Protecting plants from the weather and from marauders has always been the gardener's problem. The glass garden cloche was invented in 1623 in Italy, while the similarly shaped terracotta rhubarb forcers enjoyed great popularity in the nineteenth and early twentieth centuries in Britain. Both have become fashionable once again, with the renewed interest in 'growing your own'.

The Roman Emperor Tiberius had the first greenhouse, according to Hill in *The Gardener's Labyrinth*. 'The young plants may be defended from cold and boisterous windes,' he wrote, 'yea, frosts, the cold aire, and hot Sunne, if Glasses made for the onely purpose, be set over them, which on such wise bestowed on the beds, yeelded in a manner to Tiberius Caesar, Cucumbers all the year, in which he took great delight.'

The repeal of window taxes in the early 1800s and the technology for making glazing bars ushered in the grand era of the conservatory and the greenhouse, with Decimus Burton's Palm House, constructed in Kew Gardens in the 1840s, being the most majestic example.

Glass was used for Wardian cases, the invention of Dr Nathaniel Ward, a London physician and botanist, in 1829. These glazed cases revolutionised the work of plant finders who had previously seen precious specimens perish when sent home from overseas. One of the first people to take advantage of the new invention was Joseph Dalton Hooker, subsequently director of Kew Gardens from 1865–1885, when he shipped back live plants to England from New Zealand in 1841.

Wheelbarrows

A man wheeling a barrow is the archetypal image of the gardener. Think of Mr McGregor in Beatrix Potter's *The Tale of Peter Rabbit*, or the delicate line drawings of Eric Ravilious in his *Garden* sequence.

The first person to use a wheelbarrow in England would have lived in the twelfth century, although it's not certain whether he would have been pushing or pulling it. It's thought wheelbarrows were introduced by Crusaders from the Middle East (always ahead of us in gardening terms, as in so much else, at the time).

Originally made of wood, they were later made of steel, and the first wheelbarrow with a pneumatic tyre was introduced in about 1900. But little else has changed: I'm still wheeling my father's 1950s barrow.

Changing times

Interestingly, gardeners probably had the most extensive choice of garden tools between the First and Second World Wars. The previous century had seen an increased interest in gardening across the social classes, along with the growth of manufacturing industry. Country estates, however, continued to employ their own carpenters and blacksmiths to hand-make tools, leading to regional variations in tool design. Suffolk billhooks, for example, had front-heavy convex blades suitable for cutting rushes and sedges, while the Leicester billhook had a double-bladed, sickle-shaped edge for general work and to give a straight edge to thorn tufts.

In the late 1920s, C. T. Skelton, a Sheffield toolmaker, was still making spades, forks and other tools in regional styles, including Cheshire, Irish, Kentish, Scottish and Guernsey. A 'Canterbury' hoe, for example, was a fork with three sturdy, flattened prongs. Local spade design persisted until World War Two.

Post-war mass production, however, introduced a new level of standardisation. You can now buy your tools in many different materials, including stainless steel and injection-moulded plastics, but, ironically, they won't offer you the choice of design and regional character that our great-grandparents enjoyed less than eighty years ago.

Where to see classic tools

British Lawnmower Museum, Merseyside PR8 5AJ (01704 501336; www.lawnmowerworld.co.uk)

Garden Museum, Lambeth Bridge Road, London SE1 7LB (020 7401 8865; www.gardenmuseum.org.uk)

Top ten gardening tools
(or the tools no gardener should be without)

1. **SPADE** – well, you can't start a garden until you've dug over the soil and made a big hole for your plants.

2. **FORK** – now mostly made from stainless or carbon steel, but once made from iron.

3. **DIBBER** – once called a 'setting styke', and usually still wooden, this tool has been used since the first man gardened.

4. **TROWEL** – who can disagree with Sam Beeton, who said in his 1861 *Book of Garden Management* that it's the one tool no one can do without.

5. **HOE** – comes in all shapes and sizes, but the small-headed, D-shaped hoe is the thing for sorting out the weeds.

6. **SECATEURS** – wander out into the garden on any day of the year and there will always be something to be deadheaded, clipped back or tidied away.

7. **BULB PLANTER** – if you want any kind of spring display in your garden, you'll need to plant dozens of bulbs. Back-breaking work without a planter.

8. **LAWNMOWER** – I still hanker after my father's petrol mower when I trip over our electric mower's trailing wires from the house. Such a good finish, too.

9. **TOPIARY SHEARS** – most gardens crave winter structure which topiary provides. So a sharp pair of one-handled shears, used with skill on the box on Derby Day in June, will give you year-round interest.

10. **WHEELBARROW** – stainless steel is best really, as plastic cracks and splits. And there's now a bit of a retro fashion for wood.

10,000BCE	Humankind started gardening with mattocks, shovels and diggers
14–37CE	During Tiberius's reign, the first greenhouse was created so the emperor's cucumbers could be grown year-round
79CE	Before the eruption of Vesuvius in 79CE, the Romans at Pompeii used hoes, forks, rakes and short-handled spades. They also turned their hand to topiary with shears
Pre-Conquest England	Scythe is an Anglo-Saxon word, indicating that before the Norman Conquest, farmers and gardeners were cutting grasses and reeds with iron scythes
1100s	First wheelbarrow recorded in England, believed to have been introduced by a Crusader returning from the Middle East
1170s	A stained-glass window at Canterbury Cathedral shows Adam digging Eden with a long-handled spade
1190s	The expense and importance of garden tools are underlined by an early treatise, *De Utensilibus*, by Alexander Neckham
1259	The new lawns at the Palace of Westminster were rolled with a marble roller
1389	Early mention of hoes, spades, shovels, rakes, trowels, forks, seed baskets, sieves, rope, ladders, scythes, sickles, axes, saws and shears in an Abingdon Abbey inventory
1400s	Monks were already using conduits and lead pipes to transport water to their gardens
1580	First use of the world 'watering-pot', according to the *Oxford English Dictionary*
1623	Glass garden cloche invented in Italy
1633	First visual image of a bulb planter, in Giovanni Baptista Ferrari's *Flora*
1692	First mention of 'watering-can', again noted by the *Oxford English Dictionary*
1700	Invention of the seed drill by Jethro Tull

1827	Thomas Hancock of Fulham introduces the India rubber hose
1829	Invention of the Wardian case for transporting live plants
1830	First lawnmower patented by Edwin Budding
1854	First mechanised hedge trimmer devised in Idaho. Leaf-sweeping machines also first appeared in the mid-century
1860	First patent taken out for hedge clippers. Secateurs are probably also a nineteenth-century invention
1870s	First patent for a lawn sprinkler taken out
1893	Introduction of the first steam-powered lawnmower
1912	Invention of the powered rotary hoe on an Australian farm
1926	The invention of the chainsaw
1933	First rotary mower appeared
1950s	The introduction of injection-moulded plastic tools
1955	Invention of the first petrol-driven hedge cutter
1962	The appearance of the Flymo hover mower
1969	MowBot (which perhaps gave its name to Mo Farrah's Olympic gesture), the first commercial robotic lawnmower, was patented
1995	A fully solar-powered robotic mower became available
2000s	We're still waiting for the first great gardening invention of the twenty-first century

CHAPTER 4

THE HORTICULTURAL HALL OF FAME

The love of gardening is a seed once sown that never dies.
GERTRUDE JEKYLL (1843–1932)

As soon as you draw up any list, you spark disagreement – so making a choice of twenty-five top gardeners over the past 2,500 years is a tricky one. Here's my selection. See if you agree.

Theophrastus (c. 372–287BCE)

Hardly a household name, but you have to include the Ancient Greek botanist, Theophrastus. He studied under Aristotle, who is said to have left him his garden, and taught at the Lyceum in Athens. Author of *Historia plantarum* and *Causae plantarum*, he garnered detailed information from farmers, market gardeners and doctors, and described plants for the first time in terms of their resemblances and their differences.

Pliny the Younger (23-79CE)

The more famous Pliny has distracted attention from Theophrastus. A lawyer and cavalry officer, he was also the author of *Historia naturalis*, an encyclopaedic compendium about science, art and plants, which was influential through to the Middle Ages. His writings helped give a picture of Roman gardens.

Ogier Ghiselin de Busbecq (1521-1592)

Flemish-born herbalist and diplomat de Busbecq served as the Holy Roman Emperor's ambassador to the court of Suleiman the Magnificent in Constantinople. There, his eye was caught by the tulip which had been cultivated in the Ottoman Empire throughout the Middle Ages; he is credited with introducing this essential garden flower to western Europe.

John Gerard (1545-1612)

It was a toss-up between Gerard and William Turner (c.1508–1568), the latter being regarded as the father of English botany. But Gerard, a barber-surgeon and supervisor of Lord Burghley's London garden, squeaks in because of the overnight success of his 1597 *Herball*. Despite being error-ridden and with more than a hint of plagiarism, the herbal's clear plant descriptions were used by generations of English gardeners.

The Tradescants

John the Elder (c. 1570–1638) and his son, the Younger (1608–1662), bestride Stuart gardening like colossi. The Elder Tradescant worked for both Robert Cecil and the Duke of Buckingham, and collected plants on diplomatic and other missions to Russia, the Low Countries and North Africa. John the Younger carried on his father's nursery, and plant-hunted in Barbados and Virginia. The curiosities displayed in the Tradescants' museum at Lambeth were unscrupulously procured by Elias Ashmole, who used them to found Oxford's Ashmolean Museum.

André Le Nôtre (1613–1700)

Le Nôtre was the son of a Tuileries gardener, and his first major project was Vaux-le-Vicomte for Nicolas Fouquet, Louis XIV's finance minister. When Fouquet was arrested for embezzlement, Le Nôtre was snapped up for Versailles. He laid out formal terraces, parterres, fountains and woods, and set the gold standard for gardening in the absolutist fashion. This was the garden – and the monarchy – against which all others should be judged and found wanting.

The landscape lovers

It's a cheat, perhaps, to lump together the three leaders of the English Landscape movement, but they seem to me inseparable, representing between them the development of gardening in England over the eighteenth century. Royal and aristocratic gardener Charles Bridgeman (1690-1738) opened up landscapes at Stowe and Claremont with graceful avenues, while still retaining some formality. Trained as a painter in Rome, William Kent (1685-1748) was more gifted as a garden designer, as can be seen by comparing his ravishing outside work at Chiswick House with his inferior paintings inside. His crowning achievement is the garden at Rousham in Oxfordshire. The best known of the trio, 'Capability' Brown (1716-1783) rose from gardener's boy to the companion of dukes, travelling ceaselessly across the country and working at, among many other places, Blenheim, Bowood, Croome Court and Kew Gardens. A visionary designer, he transformed the English landscape, introducing a greater naturalism, and planting parkland trees which he would never live to see mature.

The royal gardeners

Spare a thought for a flash of royal interest in gardening (to be submerged until the Queen Mother and Prince Charles stood up to the plate in the late twentieth century). The consort of George II, Queen Caroline of Ansbach (1683-1737) worked with Bridgeman and Kent on her Richmond garden, while her eldest son, Frederick, Prince of Wales (1707-1751), gardened next door at Kew (actually wielding a spade himself). After his early death, his widow, Augusta (1719-1772), mother of George III, continued his work at Kew, creating a physic garden to 'contain all the plants known on earth', and becoming the effective founder of the Royal Botanic Gardens.

Philip Miller (1691-1771)

This Scottish market gardener's son was head gardener at the Chelsea Physic Garden in London for nearly fifty years. He made Chelsea one of the leading botanic gardens in Europe, experimenting with plants he introduced from all over the world. Miller's *Gardener's Dictionary* (1731) was a bible for eighteenth-century gardeners, and influenced the first four American presidents, Washington, Adams, Jefferson and Madison, in the planting of their estates.

Carl Linnaeus (1707–1778)

Few people have had more impact on how we describe plants than Sweden's most famous natural scientist. In 1753, he published the first edition of his *Species plantarum*, which introduced the binomial system of plant names used universally ever since. In Linnaeus's system, the *genus* name is followed by the *species* (for example, *Papaver orientale*).

Sir Joseph Banks (1743–1820)

Not a gardener per se, but a leading botanist and natural scientist, who accompanied James Cook on the *Endeavour* to Tahiti, Brazil, New Zealand and Australia. Appointed director of Kew by George III, Banks established the gardens' importance as a research institution and as a plant showcase for Britain's imperial ventures. In 1804, he founded what became the Royal Horticultural Society, in a room above Hatchard's bookshop in London's Piccadilly.

Humphrey Repton (1752-1818)

Repton took over where 'Capability' Brown left off, styling himself as a 'landscape gardener'. But he was less hands-on than his fêted predecessor, working instead as a consultant to his aristocratic clients. He presented designs in his Red Books, accompanying his text with watercolours and flaps showing before and after. As a taste for the Picturesque developed, Repton's style changed. He re-anchored the house in the garden, adding terraces, flowers and ornamentation. His design for Russell Square in London, recently restored, anticipates the Victorian fondness for greater intricacy in planting.

John Claudius Loudon (1783-1843)

J. C. Loudon's *Encyclopaedia of Gardening*, published in 1822, made his name and fortune. Effectively the first horticultural journalist (with his wife, Jane, writing about flowers), he established the monthly *Gardener's Magazine* in 1826, which aimed to 'put Gardens in distant parts of the country on a footing with those about the metropolis'. Part of his mission was to encourage his largely middle-class readership to take up gardening.

Sir Joseph Paxton (1803-1865)

By the age of twenty-three, this farm labourer's son from Bedford was already head gardener at Chatsworth, the Devonshire family's palace in Derbyshire. He acquired exotic plants from around the world, and built ranges of glasshouses in which to grow them. A self-taught engineer, he designed the Great Conservatory (demolished in 1920), with a central path wide enough for a horse-drawn carriage, and went on to design the Crystal Palace for the Great Exhibition of 1851.

William Robinson (1838-1935)

The nineteenth century's Italianate revival in gardens, with formal parterres and carpet bedding, was attacked by Irish-born gardener William Robinson, head of native plants at the Royal Botanic Society's Regent's Park gardens. In a series of books, of which *The English Flower Garden* (1883) was the most influential, he trenchantly expressed his preference for hardy plants over annuals, setting the style for the next generation's gardeners.

Gertrude Jekyll (1843-1932)

Robinson's advocacy of the relaxed cottage garden style inspired Gertrude Jekyll, as did the Arts and Crafts movement. Together with the architect Edwin Lutyens (1869–1944), she worked on more than a hundred gardens across Britain. Lutyens, using local materials, gave their gardens geometric structure, which was softened by Jekyll's planting. She used her painter's training to create drifts rather than blocks of colour, and allowed different plants and flowers to flow into one another.

Lawrence Johnston (1871-1958)

Few people had greater impact on twentieth-century English gardening than this shy Anglo-American, whose formidable mother bought the Hidcote estate in Gloucestershire in 1907. Johnston left few papers and wrote little, but his testament is the garden which he made in the decades following the First World War. Now one of the jewels in the National Trust crown, it comprises a series of rooms, each with a distinct character, contained within hedges of yew and beech.

Beatrix Farrand (1872–1959)

A niece of the novelist Edith Wharton, Farrand studied painting before becoming a landscape architect in New York. Her garden designs had a certain formality and sense of proportion, with perennial plants used with elegant restraint. Her surviving major works include Dumbarton Oaks and the campuses at Yale and Princeton.

Vita Sackville-West (1892–1962)

Author and poet Vita Sackville-West, the only daughter of Baron Sackville of Knole in Kent, was cheated out of inheriting by her sex. So she devoted herself to Sissinghurst Castle, a collection of ruined buildings which she bought with her husband, the diplomat and politician Harold Nicolson, in 1929. Influenced by Hidcote and by Persian gardens, the couple created one of the twentieth century's most famous gardens, visited by thousands every year. Harold designed the layout, and Vita filled the rooms with magical and seasonal planting combinations. At Sissinghurst's heart is the much imitated White Garden, a fantasy of all-white flowers set off by silvery-grey foliage.

Roberto Burle Marx (1909–1994)

The son of a wealthy Brazilian mother and a German father, Burle Marx is credited with introducing Modernism to Brazil, although his influence has stretched much further than his own country. He designed his first landscape in 1932, and later led expeditions into the Brazilian rainforest with botanists and landscape architects to gather plant material.

Christopher Lloyd (1921–2006)

Christopher Lloyd turned the yew-framed garden at Great Dixter, a centuries-old manor in East Sussex, into the most outstanding and well-maintained few acres in Britain. It has long herbaceous borders yielding interest all summer long, a hot-coloured garden with cannas, dahlias and spiky succulents, and wildflower meadows. Through his garden and his weekly *Country Life* column, Lloyd was a major force in British gardening over four decades.

Beth Chatto (1923–)

Beth Chatto and Lloyd published their correspondence in *Dear Friend and Gardener*, a book which became a minor gardening classic. It shed light on their different but equally rigorous approaches. Chatto made her garden out of an inhospitable site in Essex with both dry and wet areas. These conditions dictated how she gardened, which was to grow the right plant in the right place. Her style was also influenced by her interest in natural plant associations and by the painter and plantsman, Cedric Morris. In her garden and on her stands at the Chelsea Flower Show, she encouraged the use of unusual hardy perennials, enjoying their foliage texture and contrast as well as their flowers.

Piet Oudolf (1944-)

The new Bowes-Lyon Rose Garden at the Royal Horticultural Society's garden at Wisley shows the far-reaching influence of Piet Oudolf's 'New Perennial' style. Roses are planted among grasses, perennials and shrubs, a far cry from the traditional rose garden of individual blooms. The Dutch-born nurseryman, garden designer and author uses bold drifts of grasses intermingled with herbaceous perennials selected for their structure. His major projects have included the Lurie roof garden at the Millennium Park in Chicago, the Trentham estate in Staffordshire and the Walled Garden at Scampston in North Yorkshire.

Chelsea stars

The jury is still out on the Chelsea Flower Show designers most likely to wield lasting influence, so it's invidious, perhaps, to pick out a few individuals. These three Gold-medal winners all seem to me to have significantly affected how we view gardens: Tom Stuart-Smith creates gardens with native trees, and plants delicate wild flowers and hardy perennials which ripple through blocks of green meadow grass. Swedish designer Ulf Nordfjell has made several appearances at Chelsea, where his strong lines and sleek use of stone, steel and other hard materials enhance the cool sophistication of his textural planting. Cleve West, like Pope, consults the genius of the place, and plants accordingly, with an awareness of biodiversity. He uses his plants architecturally, leaving space between them to show off their shape.

Television quartet

Gardeners' World, British television's leading garden programme, has had several presenters over the years since its first broadcast in 1968. Four stand out as having both reflected and led gardening in their time. Percy Thrower (1913–1988) was the gardener who rolled up his sleeves, used chemicals, planted annuals and had everything neat and tidy, in the fashion of the 1960s and 70s. Down-to-earth, cost-conscious Geoff Hamilton (1936–1996) shared both his successes and failures with his audience and stressed the importance of organic gardening. Alan Titchmarsh (1949–), the ubiquitous man of British television, a parks gardener turned Kew-trainee, caught the zeitgeist by also devising *Ground Force*, a programme offering instant garden makeovers. But his commentary was never less than authoritative. Ladies' pin-up and former jeweller Monty Don (1955–) has had two spells at the *GW* helm. His interest lies in a more naturalistic style of gardening in keeping with today's horticultural fashions.

Ten all-time top gardeners

Tales of plant-hunting derring-do

Taken along by his boss, the Duke of Buckingham, **John Tradescant the Elder** dodged the bullets at the siege of the Ile de Re in 1627, and managed even to do a spot of botanising.

Kew Gardens' first official plant collector, **Francis Masson**, hid in a hut overnight from a potentially murderous party of escaped 'Hottentot' convicts in South Africa in 1773.

The mutiny on the *Bounty* in 1789 was caused by Captain Bligh giving water to the breadfruit he was carrying to the West Indies for Banks rather than to his sailors.

In 1797, the dauntless **Francis Masson** was further shaken by being captured by French privateers and imprisoned for several weeks with barely enough food and water.

In 1834, **David Douglas**, the introducer to the UK of many plants including the Douglas fir and the Sitka spruce, fell into a bull pit in Hawaii and was gored to death by its occupant.

In 1886, French priest **Father Jean Marie Delavay**, discoverer of the blue poppy, *Meconopsis betonicifolia*, caught bubonic plague while plant hunting in Yunnan in China and never recovered his health.

Ernest 'Lily' Wilson is so called because he found the royal lily, *Lilium regale*, in a rocky crevice in China. Thrown hundreds of feet down the mountain by a landslide, he was left with a lifelong limp to remind him of his discovery.

Reginald Farrer, the father of British rock gardening, spent years hunting alpines in China but was finally defeated by the climate of the unexplored mountains of Upper Burma in 1920.

CHAPTER 5

GARDEN VISITING

Kew Gardens will be open every Thursday, for the Reception of such Persons as chuse to walk in them; and none are to be refused admission who make a decent Appearance.

LONDON DAILY ADVERTISER, 1772

Gardens have always been for show, which suggests that gardens have always been for visiting. There are a few – but very few – people who garden away privately without wanting anyone else to admire the fruits of their labours. Visit any gardener's home and the first question will be, 'Would you like to see the garden?', followed hard on its heels by the inevitable, 'You should have been here last week'. That's possibly why the Romans and their successors in the Renaissance went in for fountains, stone terraces and topiary, to make a year-round impression.

Medieval monasteries

Before 1536, when Henry VIII decided to dissolve every monastery in England and Wales, the monks had provided accommodation and food to both pilgrims and other travellers. These visitors would have benefited from the vegetables, herbs and fruit grown in the monastery gardens. They would no doubt have taken a turn themselves in the gardens, and by so doing spread knowledge about plants, planting and herbal remedies around the countryside. The style of gardening hinted at in the plays of Shakespeare suggests that the Warwickshire villagers may well have learned much from the monks' expertise.

Renaissance gardens

The medieval garden was a place of retreat and contemplation. Not so the Renaissance garden, which harked back to the values of ancient Rome to impress upon visitors the power, brilliance and wealth of its creators. It is unlikely that the general public had much access to the gardens made by the Medici family in and around Florence, but Lorenzo the Magnificent certainly entertained poets, artists, writers and philosophers at the Villa Medici at Fiesole in the late fifteenth century. The Boboli Gardens, behind the Palazzo Pitti in the city of Florence itself, still a haven of shady walks and statues and now open daily, were a centre for Cosimo de Medici's botanical interests, visited by scientists from across Europe.

Palazzo Piccolomini, built in 1459 by Pope Pius II in his home town, Pienza, in Tuscany, had terraces with geometric flowerbeds surrounding fountains and was ornamented with bushes clipped into cones and spheres. It was open to view, so that the townspeople could look up from below at the success of their local hero.

Royal progresses

Both Henry VIII and his daughter, Elizabeth I, enjoyed journeying around England and putting their nobles to maximum inconvenience. A visit to Penshurst in Kent by Henry VIII in the early 1520s convinced the king that its owner, the third Duke of Buckingham, was too wealthy for his own good. The duke was arrested, tried and executed.

In May 1583, Elizabeth visited Theobalds, the Hertfordshire house of her first minister, William Cecil, Lord Burghley. A member of the Manners family wrote: 'She was never in any place better pleased, and sure the house, garden and walks may compare with any delicate place in Italy.' Although she had never been in Italy herself, this was a compliment on the high fashion of Theobalds.

Interrupted by war

The turmoil caused by civil war and the austerity of the Commonwealth years put paid to the creation of rich gardens but not entirely to garden visiting. The royalist diarist and gardener John Evelyn, author of the seminal work on trees, *Sylva* (1664), spent periods of exile visiting gardens in Europe. He visited the Villa d'Este at Tivoli near Rome in May 1645, writing about the expense and lavishness of the gardens: 'In the Garden at the right hand are plac'd 16 vast Conchas of marble jetting out Waters… not far from that 4 sweete & delicious Gardens; descending thence two pyramids of Water, &… a Grove of trees neere it… The Whole said to have Cost the best part of a Million'.

Back in England during the Commonwealth, his account of 'a Journey into the Northern parts' in 1654 suggests that houses and gardens were by then open, at least occasionally, to the general public. Among other places, Evelyn visited '*Welbeck* the house of the *Marquis* of *New-castle*, seated in a botome in a Prk, & invirond with Woods, a noble, yet melancholy seate'.

Forty years later, Celia Fiennes, the daughter of a Cromwellian colonel, also visited Welbeck, its owner by then a Duke and clearly profiting from the Restoration and renewed access to European influences. 'The gardens are very neate,' she wrote, 'and after the London Mode, of Gravel and Grass Walks and Mount, and the Squaires with dwarfes and Cyprus ffirse and all sorts of Greens and fruite trees, holly trees, box and ffilleroy [phillyrea] ffinely cut.'

Whig wonders

The eighteenth century saw a sudden rise in tourism. As early as 1717, Lord Cobham opened the New Inn as a centre for paying visitors to Stowe. The public rang a bell at the gate for admission, and were then shown around along a pre-determined route. Henry Hoare, the owner of Stourhead in Wiltshire, like Cobham, also built a hotel for visitors to his garden – the most visited National Trust attraction today.

The first ever garden guidebooks were published on Stowe in 1745, and reprinted regularly into the nineteenth century. The public were there on sufferance, and were never admitted when the family was at home. Even a fellow aristocrat, Viscount Torrington, could not gain admission when Cobham's great-nephew was in residence later in the century. 'The Mss of Buckingham is return'd to Stowe,' he wrote, 'else we had thoughts of surveying it.'

Other, smaller gardens were equally popular. The diarist Horace Walpole restricted the number of visitors to his celebrated garden at Strawberry Hill by issuing pre-booked tickets.

> *Visitor numbers*
>
> *Nearly 20,000 more people visited Stowe in 2012 than 2011 after the re-opening of Cobham's 1717 New Inn as a visitor centre in March 2012.*

Queues at Kew

The royal gardens at Kew and Richmond (since the early nineteenth century, united as Kew Gardens) have always been open to the public. When Queen Caroline gardened there with Bridgeman and Kent in the 1720s and 1730s, she employed a rustic poet, Stephen Duck, to live in the Hermitage, while his wife, Sarah, explained the elaborate conceits of Merlin's Cave to visitors.

Sightseers were shown around by servants, inclined at times to throw their weight about. In 1765 a gentleman was denied entry to Kew by the doorkeeper who 'chose rather to wait on a group of his own stamp… composed of house-maids, cooks, grooms, etc.', while the agricultural writer and observer, Arthur Young, witnessed a similar incident of 'excessive insolence' at Blenheim in 1768. In the 1770s, a man subsequently placed in a madhouse defaced trees at Kew, prompting George III to consider closing the gardens to the public. He relented, and from 1772 the gardens remained open.

Victorian voyages

Garden visiting grew apace in the nineteenth century. In 1849, a party from Sheffield visited Chatsworth on a tour organised by a temperance worker called Thomas Cook, whose son founded the eponymous travel business. A reporter for the *Derbyshire Courier* described the day, saying that 'Through the condescension and kindness of the noble Duke of Devonshire, the excursionists were … permitted to visit the splendid gardens and pleasure grounds. Between 4,000 and 5,000 were… believed promenading in the park, in the palace, and in the pleasure-grounds of Chatsworth.'

Royal visitors still came at a cost. Queen Victoria and Prince Albert visited in 1843, giving the Duke of Devonshire only three weeks' notice. Highlight of the visit was Paxton's Great Conservatory, which had cost a fantastic £33,099. The queen wrote that it was 'the most stupendous and extraordinary creation imaginable'. The following year, for a proposed visit to Chatsworth of Tsar Nicholas I of Russia, Paxton built the majestic Emperor Fountain, with a jet shooting up 264 feet (80 metres). The emperor never came.

An expensive visit

A visit to Stowe by Queen Victoria and Prince Albert in 1845 destroyed the fortunes of the Duke of Buckingham. Two years later, his effects were seized by bailiffs and he fled abroad.

Public parks

In his monthly *Gardener's Magazine*, John Loudon encouraged enthusiastic gardeners to visit other gardens to glean ideas for their own, although what the general public learned from the Emperor Fountain and the Great Conservatory at Chatsworth is hard to guess. Paxton, however, laid out the first public park in Birkenhead, after which many other towns followed suit.

A turn in the park after Sunday lunch became an accepted form of recreation, with the public able to admire acres of the fashionable carpet bedding. Dozens of gardeners were employed to lay out these beds, so park gardening became one of the chief forms of training for the next century or so.

National Gardens Scheme

Until the late 1920s, garden visiting was restricted to public parks and large estates. Then, in 1927 the redoubtable Miss Elsie Wagg dreamt up the idea of the National Gardens Scheme to raise funds for the Queen's Nursing Institute. Over 600 gardens opened under the scheme for days in June, July and August that first year. They included the great and the grand, such as Sandringham, the king's Norfolk home, and Blenheim. But William Robinson also opened his garden at Gravetye in Sussex and the Honourable Mrs Portman showed off the best of modern design at her Jekyll garden at Hestercombe in Somerset. Increasingly, other, smaller gardens began to open under the scheme, which in 2012 donated £2.6 million to a variety of charities. Now nearly 4,000 gardens are listed annually in the famous *Yellow Book*, which has become an invaluable reference for thousands of garden visitors.

The Yellow Book

Gardeners wishing to have their gardens included in the Yellow Book *undergo a rigorous assessment by a member of the county organising team. Assessors are looking for a high standard of horticulture, and plenty to interest a range of visitors. Gardeners will sometimes be encouraged to try again the following year if the garden is still too much a work in progress. Many gardens continue to open year after year: 82 gardens which opened for the NGS in 1927 are opening for the scheme in 2014.*

For many garden openers, part of the delight of the scheme is the chance to talk to other enthusiastic gardeners. Vita Sackville-West often shunned company, yet enjoyed the visits to Sissinghurst of the people she called her 'shillingses' (a shilling or 5p being the price of admission in the 1930s when she first opened). She wrote in the *New Statesman* in 1939 about 'these mild, gentle men and women... these homely souls who will travel fifty miles by bus with a fox-terrier on a lead, who will pore over a label, taking notes in a penny notebook – these are some of the people I most gladly welcome and salute.'

The big guns

By the twenty-first century, visits to garden centres and gardens had become among Britain's chief relaxations. Three of the National Trust's top five visitor attractions in 2012 were the gardens of Stourhead in Wiltshire, Wakehurst Place in West Sussex, and Cliveden in Berkshire. The Royal Horticultural Society, with 400,000 members by 2013, was given the estate at Wisley by Sir Thomas Hanbury in 1903. The society turned the house into a laboratory and offices, while the garden was developed as a mixture of pleasure and trial grounds, open from the beginning to the public. It was another eighty-four years before the RHS acquired another garden (Rosemoor in Devon), but it has since taken on Hyde Hall in Essex (1993) and Harlow Carr in Yorkshire (2007). The stepping up of the pace of acquisition is suggestive of public interest in gardening and garden visiting.

And visitors still throng to Britain's flagship garden, the World Heritage Site of the Royal Botanic Gardens, Kew. Well over one million people passed through its turnstiles in 2012. When deciding to continue opening in 1772, George III made a good call.

Open gardens

Fifteen NGS 1927 garden openers still opening in 2013

Abbotsbury Gardens, Dorset

Arley Hall, Cheshire

Batsford Arboretum, Gloucestershire

Blickling Hall, Norfolk

Broughton Castle, Oxfordshire

Erddig Hall, Clwyd

Great Dixter, East Sussex

Hestercombe, Somerset

Hodnet Hall Gardens, Shropshire

Lanhydrock House, Cornwall

Melbourne Hall, Derbyshire

Newby Hall, North Yorkshire

Ramster, Surrey

Sandringham, Norfolk

Trewithen, Cornwall

Equipment every UK garden visitor needs

Handbooks (the *NGS Yellow Book*, Scotland's *Gardens Guide*, the National Trust and English Heritage Handbooks)

Stout shoes (the lawns may need aerating, but the gardeners would probably appreciate your not doing it in high heels)

Waterproofs (there's no such thing as bad weather; just the wrong clothing)

A notebook and pen (Penelope Hobhouse would refuse to give plant names to visitors who asked for a pen or pulled out a cheque stub on which to write when visiting her garden at Tintinhull in Somerset)

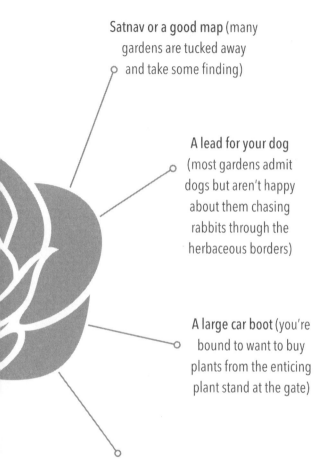

Satnav or a good map (many gardens are tucked away and take some finding)

A lead for your dog (most gardens admit dogs but aren't happy about them chasing rabbits through the herbaceous borders)

A large car boot (you're bound to want to buy plants from the enticing plant stand at the gate)

A good appetite (especially if you're visiting NGS gardens which tend to serve celestial lemon drizzle cake)

CHAPTER 6

GARDENS OF THE WORLD

Forty gardens you must see and why

> *One is nearer God's heart in a garden*
> *Than anywhere else on earth.*
> DOROTHY GURNEY (1858–1912)

This chapter offers just a taster of the many thousands of gardens open to the public worldwide. It is very partial and omits many countries, but I hope it will whet the appetite of gardeners and garden visitors to explore further afield.

United Kingdom

Abbey House Gardens, Malmesbury, Wiltshire

If you want to get back to Eden then visit these gardens on one of the half dozen Clothes Optional Days during the year. Clad or unclad, the uninhibited owners, Ian and Barbara Pollard, have planted 2,000 roses, 50,000 tulips, smothered the house with fragrant climbers and created a Celtic Cross knot garden.

The Alnwick Garden, Northumberland

The twenty-first century's first grand garden, the brainchild of the Duchess of Northumberland has turned a quiet corner of northern England into a tourist Mecca (helped by Alnwick Castle being a film location for Harry Potter). Its Grand Cascade is the bold centrepiece, but there are also ornamental, rose and poison gardens.

The Beth Chatto Gardens, Essex

Starting in 1960 with an overgrown wasteland, Beth Chatto has created one of the most celebrated gardens of recent years. Its boggy and dry conditions mean that this is a garden of contrasts, with plant-fringed ponds, woodland, a Mediterranean garden and a now legendary gravel garden on the site of a former car park.

Biddulph Grange, Staffordshire

Biddulph is a monument to high Victorian style. It has a 500-foot (150-metre) dahlia walk, Chinese temple and bridge, Italianate terraces, parterres and rockeries. Within its framework of hedges, walls and screens are trees and shrubs introduced from Italy, Scotland, China and Japan.

Bodnant Garden, Conwy

Famed for its collection of rhododendron hybrids, this garden was made by five generations of the same family and has uninterrupted views of Snowdonia. Sweeping lawns, a 180-foot (55-m) laburnum tunnel and an eighteenth-century garden pavilion are highlights. A succession of terraces lead down to the richly planted Dell Garden.

Chelsea Physic Garden, London

Tucked away from the bustle of nearby King's Road, the Chelsea Physic has the charm of a private garden. Internationally renowned, it was founded in 1673 by the Apothecaries' Society, and holds about 5,000 plant collections, including Mediterranean, sub-tropical and tropical species.

Chiswick House Garden, London

Regarded as the cradle of the English Landscape Movement, these elegant gardens around Lord Burlington's rotunda at Chiswick were laid out in the 1720s and were one of William Kent's earliest projects. The recently restored conservatory houses a 200-year-old camellia collection, at its peak in March.

East Ruston Old Vicarage Garden, Norfolk

This out-of-the-way but highly theatrical Norfolk garden has a succession of styles to suit every taste, with green corridors of beech, holm oaks and acacia, dividing lines of topiary, box-edged parterres, woodland areas, and Mediterranean, sub-tropical, desert and exotic gardens.

Eden Project, Cornwall

Fresh from rescuing the Lost Gardens of Heligan, the enterprising Tim Smit turned his hand to creating different exotic gardens within a series of biodomes in a disused Cornish quarry. The emphasis is on education, and fostering an understanding of the importance of plants.

Great Dixter, East Sussex

This lovely garden wraps itself around a medieval manor house, restored and extended by Edwin Lutyens in 1910. It has a series of different linked areas, framed by yew hedging and including the sheltered Sunken Garden, Exotic Garden, orchard meadow and the famous Long Border, densely planted like a closely woven tapestry.

Hampton Court Palace, Surrey

These royal gardens reflect over 300 years of gardening history. Charles II laid out the *patte d'oie* (radiating avenues) and the Long Water in imitation of his first cousin's Versailles. The Privy Garden, with gravel and miniature topiary, and the Great Maze were the work of King William III and Queen Mary II in the late seventeenth century, while later additions include the 1768 Great Vine, a sunken garden with carpet bedding, and the secluded, shrubby Twentieth-Century Garden.

Hidcote, Gloucestershire

Modernism meets cottage gardening at Lawrence Johnston's Hidcote, which has open green spaces, as well as densely planted garden rooms separated by hornbeam and yew hedging. It is inward-looking, yet sudden, unexpected views of the Vale of Evesham can be glimpsed, for example, along the axis of the pleached hornbeam hedging of the Stilt Garden (trees with branches interwoven at above head height). Other delights include the dazzling double Red Border, the Pillar Garden, the Rock Bank, and the White and Old Gardens.

Inverewe, Wester Ross

Created out of bare rock in the 1860s, this remote Scottish woodland garden benefits from the Gulf Stream. Despite being as far north as St Petersburg, it is planted with colourful and exotic plants such as Himalayan poppies, Tasmanian eucalyptus, Chinese rhododendrons and the most northerly planting of Wollemi pines.

Mount Stewart, County Down

Sub-tropical plants thrive here thanks to the garden's sheltered position by Strangford Lough. Outstanding is the 1920s Italian Garden, with bold palm trees, red hot pokers, day lilies and cannas. Don't miss the Shamrock Garden with the Irish harp in yew and the Red Hand of Ulster, planted with red-leafed begonias.

Royal Botanic Garden, Edinburgh

With panoramic views towards Edinburgh Castle, this major research centre holds one of the world's largest plant collections. Visitors can roam through ten different climactic zones in the historic glasshouses, and also enjoy the rock garden, peat wall, Chinese hillside, herbaceous borders and autumn colour in the arboretum.

Royal Botanic Gardens, Kew, Surrey

A world centre of plant science and conservation, with an historic herbarium, Kew is also the most visited garden in the UK. Open daily, the garden's highlights include wide avenues, an arboretum, Holly Walk, the massive Victorian Palm House, William Chambers' Orangery, the late twentieth-century Princess of Wales Conservatory and the new tree-top walk.

Royal Horticultural Society Garden, Wisley, Surrey

The flagship garden of the Royal Horticultural Society, Wisley combines serious horticultural experimentation, such as annual plant trials, with accessible delights for the general public, including its double herbaceous borders and cottage garden. Recent developments include the replanting of the rose garden and new greenhouse, surrounded by drift planting by Tom Stuart-Smith.

Sissinghurst Castle, Kent

Plantswoman Vita Sackville-West filled in the structure of rooms drawn up by her husband, Harold Nicolson, to create one of England's finest gardens. The epitome of cottage-garden style, its joys includes a nuttery, herb garden, Lime Walk with spring bulbs, fragrant beds of roses, and the magical White Garden.

Stourhead, Wiltshire

A choice of walks wind round the lake which is at the heart of this eighteenth-century landscape. Set in the parkland are various temples, including Alfred's Tower, an example of the Georgian obsession with Alfred the Great. The most visited National Trust property remains 'a living work of art' as it was described when it first opened to the public in the 1740s.

Stowe, Buckinghamshire

Stretching over 250 acres (101 hectares), with a further 750 acres (303 hectares) of parkland, Stowe represents every stage of the English Landscape Movement and is full of political symbolism. This may be lost on visitors today, but they can still admire its monuments and temples, and the confidence and beauty of its groves of beech, ash and oak, lakes, open views and shrubberies.

Trentham Estate, Staffordshire

Trentham offers a crash course in gardening over the last 250 years. Landscaped by 'Capability' Brown in 1759, the gardens were added to in opulent Italian style by Sir Charles Barry in the 1830s. Derelict for years, they have been rescued by designers including Tom Stuart-Smith and Piet Oudolf, who have reinterpreted the Italian Flower Garden, and put in contemporary perennial planting.

France

Giverny, Haute-Normandie

Monet's Normandy garden is familiar from a thousand reproductions of the wisteria-covered Japanese bridge over the lily pond. This is only part of the garden, however, as the rest of it lies across a railway line. A *Grande Allée* runs down from the house, flanked by flowerbeds, planted in an Impressionistic mélange of colourful climbers, perennials and annuals.

Jardins du Prieuré d'Orsan, Maisonnais

These late twentieth-century gardens work in perfect harmony with the ancient priory they surround. Leading off what is now a hotel, a hornbeam cloister frames cruciform beds planted with immaculate cabbages. Also referring back to the building's past are a kitchen garden, a medicinal herbarium, an orchard and an enclosed rose garden devoted to the Virgin Mary.

Les Jardins des Paradis, Midi-Pyrénées

Situated on a terraced hillside in the former Cathar stronghold of Cordes-sur-Ciel, these gardens have been described by one visitor as having 'plants on speed'. Everything is given a contemporary twist, with a cloister created out of bamboo and broken slates, and a cascade created by water running down through stepped metal buckets. There's a banana grove and a modern experimental potager.

Versailles, Paris

No visit to Paris is complete without a trip to Versailles, home of Louis XIV, the Sun King. The absolute monarch employed André Le Nôtre to create a garden to match, and his work is still awe-inspiring today, with its fountains, groves and orangerie. The Hall of Mirrors looks out along the main vista over the rigidly geometrical Water Parterre and the Grand Canal.

Italy

Giardino di Boboli, Florence

Originally designed in 1549 for Duke Cosimo I de' Medici on a steep hill behind the Palazzo Pitti, the Boboli Gardens showcase the Renaissance, Mannerist and Baroque periods of Italian garden history. Behind the palace is a seventeenth-century stepped amphitheatre, from which dappled walks lead to a grand Mannerist grotto.

Villa Cimbrone, Ravello

This early twentieth-century garden, designed by an Englishman with local help, has flower gardens, temples, statues, a grotto and a Moorish loggia. But the unforgettable moment is when you walk out through a Doric temple and on to a terrace suspended 1,000 feet (300 metres) up above the glittering waters of the Gulf of Salerno.

Villa d'Este, Lazio

The garden of the Villa d'Este was built in the late sixteenth century for one of Rome's richest cardinals. It is a flamboyant, allegorical, high Renaissance garden with elaborate fountains, all recently restored, as well as a labyrinth, grottoes, statues, and cascades.

The Netherlands

Keukenhof, Zuid-Holland

The gardens at Keukenhof epitomise what everyone associates with gardening in the Netherlands – bulbs. Over seven million bulbs, including 1,000 tulip varieties, are planted each year, peaking between March and May. Tulips, daffodils, crown imperials and crocuses flow in vast and colourful swathes through the landscape, and beneath avenues of trees.

Het Loo, Apeldoorn

Known as the Versailles of the Netherlands, Het Loo's strict symmetry owed much to the French style. But William of Orange's Baroque Garden is on a smaller scale, and is best viewed from the low surrounding banks. It influenced both the Privy Garden at Hampton Court and the water garden at Westbury Court in Gloucestershire.

Russia

Peterhof, St Petersburg

Versailles was the inspiration for Peter the Great's Peterhof, started in the early eighteenth century. A formal garden lies in front of the palace, behind which is the Grand Cascade, a dazzling spectacle of fountains and gold statuary. Its open vista down on to the Gulf of Finland is symbolic of St Petersburg as Russia's window onto Europe.

Spain

Los Jardines de Alfabia, Mallorca

You are never far from the sound of water in these lush Moorish gardens in the heart of Mallorca's Tramuntana range. There are contrasts between clipped hedging and a jungle of palms, bamboos and bulrushes. An ivy-covered pergola of seventy-two columns leads to a circular basin, beyond which are stepped paths down to an arena of soaring Chusan palms.

El Generalife, Andalucia

These gardens date from the early fourteenth century, like those at the nearby Alhambra. The Court of the Long Pond is flanked on three sides by buildings, with a long, thin channel of water at its centre. The space here and in other areas of the garden is divided by hedges, and colour is provided by flowers in containers and climbers on the walls.

United States Of America

Fort Worth Botanical Garden, Texas

This 109-acre (44-hectare) botanic garden has an unexpectedly wide range of planting for a state one tends to associate with hot, dry weather. There's an Italian-inspired rose garden, a perennial garden through which runs a fern-lined brook and a scented garden. But it's worth a visit for the seven-acre (2.8-hectare) Japanese garden alone, which brilliantly encapsulates the variety of Japanese styles.

Huntington Botanical Gardens, California

The Huntington Library owns works by Shakespeare and Milton, and the papers from Stowe. It also has a remarkable 100-acre (40-hectare) garden, divided into twelve areas. A rose garden planted in 1908 traces the evolution of the shrub, while a ten-acre (4-hectare) desert garden features over 4,000 species. The classical China garden has a lake surrounded by pavilions, seasonal gardens and a teahouse.

Monticello, Virginia

Using native species, Thomas Jefferson expanded and developed his estate at Monticello until his death in 1826. Over the following century, the garden virtually disappeared, but the winding flower borders and lawns were restored in the 1940s using Jefferson's own painstaking records. His vegetable garden has also now been replanted using heritage seeds.

Mount Vernon, Virginia

If you want to understand America's first president, visit his Virginian estate, bounded by the Potomac River. The gracefully symmetrical plantings feature trees and shrubs gathered from the forest on Washington's estate, representing for him the liberty which his country had won from Britain. The flower garden was a particular source of pride, with species collected from all over the world.

Barbados

Andromeda Gardens

Started in 1954 by Iris Bannochie, the six-acre (2.4-hectare) gardens are perched on the top of a limestone hillside overlooking the ocean. A stream bubbles through the centre of the garden, forming pools and waterfalls. Planting includes several varieties of orchids, palms, ferns, heliconia, hibiscus, bougainvillea, begonias and cacti, all mixing together in an abundant tapestry of colour and texture.

Brazil

Sitio Roberto Burle Marx, Rio de Janeiro

Roberto Burle Marx was a plantsman as well as a landscape designer, as can be seen from his own garden in Rio de Janeiro, where he lived for twenty years until his death in 1994. There is a sense that the Brazilian jungle is only just kept at bay as lush plantings of over 3,500 species are combined in stagey patterns around a series of open spaces.

Mexico

Las Pozas, San Luis Potosí

In 1962, eccentric British multimillionaire Edward James started work on a garden in Mexico, inspired in part by his friendship with surrealists Dalí and Magritte. 'Pure megalomania' was how James described his work, which is a fantasy of outrageous concrete structures and sculptures, many imitating the plants and creatures of the surrounding jungle.

Ten outstanding gardens

..... Best view (over the Gulf of Salerno)

..... Grandest (run a close second by Peterhof)

..... Oldest (early fourteenth century)

..... Most surreal

..... Most wacky

..... World Heritage Site garden

..... Most political

..... Most northerly

..... Most naked (for visitors and owners alike)

..... Newest (first great twenty-first-century garden)

Open gardens

Top ten National Trust gardens – numbers of visitors in 2012–2013

Over 20 million visitors paid to enter National Trust properties in the financial year 2012/2013. Here are ten top properties which are primarily visited for their gardens:

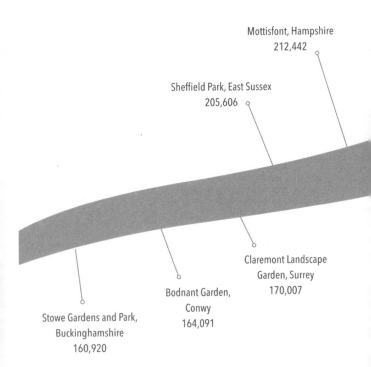

Mottisfont, Hampshire
212,442

Sheffield Park, East Sussex
205,606

Claremont Landscape
Garden, Surrey
170,007

Bodnant Garden,
Conwy
164,091

Stowe Gardens and Park,
Buckinghamshire
160,920

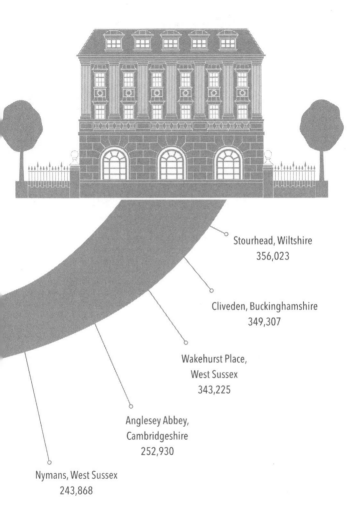

Stourhead, Wiltshire
356,023

Cliveden, Buckinghamshire
349,307

Wakehurst Place,
West Sussex
343,225

Anglesey Abbey,
Cambridgeshire
252,930

Nymans, West Sussex
243,868

CHAPTER 7

GARDENING TO WIN

Gardening is the purest of human pleasures.
FRANCIS BACON (1561–1626)

The English philosopher and statesman, Francis Bacon, took a somewhat rarefied view of gardening in his 1625 essay, *Of Gardens*. Gardening, he suggested, is a pure pleasure, refreshing the spirits of man. That's probably true, but I wonder if gardening is really as pure as all that. It seems to me that competition is endemic in gardening, as in most spheres of human endeavour. We enjoy the physical and aesthetic pleasures of gardening, but there is always the sneaky thrill of seeing whether your snowdrops/tulips/roses flower first, whether your lawn is the smoothest, whether your apples are the juiciest and most prolific. In some arenas, like the Chelsea Flower Show, the competition among designers is red in tooth and claw. A recent Gold medallist was so furious at not also winning the accolade of Best in Show that he complained in the press about the insensitivity and stupidity of the judges. In this chapter, we take a look at ways in which gardeners compete.

Tulip fever

Gambling is a form of competition, really, so we can include the extraordinary flurry of tulipomania which flared up in the 1630s. Having thrown off the Spanish yoke, and set up the Dutch East India Company, the Netherlands enjoyed golden years, with wealthy merchants spending fantastic sums on houses and gardens, and planting acres of tulips. Introduced from Turkey, the tulip was a symbol of success and status, like a Maserati today. Between 1634 and 1637, tulip bulbs changed hands like stocks and shares, and for eye-watering sums. At one point, a bulb of 'Admiral van Enkhuijsen' sold for 5,400 guilders, equal to what an Amsterdam bricklayer would earn over fifteen years. Even when the fiercest flurry of trading was over in the 1640s, the rare red-and-white striped 'Semper Augustus' still sold at 1,200 guilders a bulb (about three times the average annual pay of a Dutch worker at that time).

Political competition

Competition in gardening comes in all different shapes and sizes. The English Landscape Movement in the eighteenth century was, in a way, born out of competition, as the nation's leaders employed Charles Bridgeman, William Kent and 'Capability' Brown to enhance their estates and prove to their peers and to the general public their owners' fitness to govern. This more open style was a reaction against the excessive rigidity of Baroque French garden design and represented the liberties of the British and their triumph over French absolutism. Top of the pile was Stowe, in Buckinghamshire, the home of Lord Cobham, one of the architects of the Hanoverian succession. Every leafy walk, building, temple and statue on his estate was there to underline that the constitutional monarch only ruled courtesy of the Whig peerage.

Royalty at war

There was competition even among the royal family itself. Queen Caroline, wife of George II, employed Bridgeman and Kent at her Richmond gardens in the 1720s and 1730s. She decorated the Hermitage with busts of Isaac Newton and John Locke to align herself with Enlightenment thinking, and her weird Merlin's Cave with figures of Elizabeth of York and Elizabeth I, queens who had brought peace and unity to England. At loggerheads with Caroline, Frederick, Prince of Wales, moved in next door at Kew, and began gardening there and at his London house, to beat his mother at her own game. His iconographic figures were also heroes from English history: King Arthur and the Black Prince (Fred tempted fate by invoking a Prince of Wales who predeceased his father as he was to do).

Victorian one-upmanship

Victorian gardening wasn't just about colour and style. Epic acres of carpet bedding, elaborate rock gardens and the planting of mature trees all spelt out wealth and success. Look at any restored Victorian garden, like Biddulph in Staffordshire, or Cragside in Northumberland, and you'll get the point. At Cragside, the self-made industrialist Sir William Armstrong, keen to keep up with his aristocratic neighbour, the Duke of Northumberland, laid down massive beds of annual planting, and planted woodland trees through craggy crevasses on his estate.

The produce show

Many villages still have their annual produce shows, with competitive classes for fruit and vegetables, based on size, taste and uniformity of shape. The origins of these shows lie centuries back in the formation in the sixteenth century of florists' clubs which aimed to breed new varieties and good specimens from a particular range of plants. Competition was inherent. *The Florist's Director*, published in 1792, listed rules for plant display and judging.

On the move

The advent of the railways in the early nineteenth century saw stationmasters competing to have the best station, while other gardeners used the railways to take their prize produce to competitions across the country.

Competition in the local village show has always been stiff. Witness the Second World War film *Mrs Miniver*, in which the lady of the manor, at a dewy-eyed Greer Garson's hint, reluctantly hands the cup she's accustomed to win to the stationmaster whose rose is clearly the more deserving. A scene, incidentally, reprised in *Downton Abbey*, with Maggie Smith (Lady Grantham) yielding the prize.

There are still no holds barred. In 2011, seventy-three-year-old David Stirzaker was asked not to enter his produce in the annual North Cadbury and District Horticultural Society show in Somerset, having previously won twelve cups in four years for his carrots, parsnips and tomatoes.

Members of the National Vegetable Society also continue to compete annually with jumbo vegetables. Newark-based Peter Glazebrook has broken records for parsnips and beetroots, and holds the current world record for the largest onion (18 lb 1 oz/8.2 kg), set at the 2012 Harrogate Autumn Show.

Cops and cabbages

Medwyn Williams, then chairman of the National Vegetable Society, was pulled over by traffic police in 2010 on his way from Anglesey to a Dundee horticultural show. The cops complained that his giant onions, marrows, leeks and carrots had made his van unsafe.

RHS London shows

The Royal Horticultural Society supports gardeners and gardening in the UK and further afield. It is also at the competitive heart of horticulture, running regular shows in Westminster throughout the year, since the early twentieth century. Originally, as at Chelsea, the main exhibitors were the head gardeners of great estates displaying their produce, and nurseries showing new cultivars. But amateurs also wanted to take part, so competition classes for their produce were introduced. Exhibitors still include estates such as Blenheim and Chatsworth (the Dukes of Marlborough and Devonshire are hotly competitive about their grapes), as well as amateurs from across the UK. Size is not the only criterion: freshness and uniformity are as important, for example, when judging 'three uniform specimens of courgettes'.

Britain in bloom

Britain in Bloom, which has been organised by the RHS since 2002, was conceived in 1963 by the British Tourist Board, and inspired by the Fleurissement de France. The competition can be entered by cities, towns and villages, with categories for different sizes. This annual campaign often helps revive deprived communities, with its encouragement of general participation – for every window box, garden and park is likely to be scrutinized by the judges. In recent years, the emphasis has also been on sustainable management of the local environment. Lytham in Lancashire won the 2013 Champion of Champions award, for both its floral displays and community commitment.

Garden of the year

For generations, the press has seen competitive gardening as a way of whipping up interest and anchoring readers to their periodical. *The Daily Telegraph*, *The Times* and the *Daily Mail* have all run 'Garden of the Year' competitions over the year, as have magazines such as *The English Garden*. Winners will always tell you modestly that it was a friend who suggested that they should enter, and that they almost missed the deadline, etc. etc. But, nevertheless, something inspired hosts of amateur gardeners to send off their snaps, plans and descriptions. It's been worthwhile: more than one winner of *The Times* competition has since become a professional designer. The *Daily Mail* Garden of the Year Competition in 2013 attracted over 2,000 entries. The winner was Corinne Layton, whose choice of what she calls 'bruised colours' (black, grey and lavender) and her emphasis on form and texture are very much in the modern idiom – and light years away from the multi-coloured gardens which would have cleaned up in the past.

Garden shows

For amateurs wanting to become professionals, or for professionals seeking to raise their profile, exhibiting at a garden show is one, often rather expensive, way to do it. There are shows all over the world, including the annual Philadelphia Flower Show in the United States each March, the Bundesgartenschauen in Germany, and the International Garden Festival at Chaumont in the Loire, which runs from April to October. Since 1992, the festival's thirty or so gardens, chosen from over three hundred submissions, have become a showcase for modern design. In 2013, entries came from China, Russia, Japan and Algeria, as well as from France and the rest of Europe.

In the UK, would-be garden designers often progress through the other RHS shows at Malvern, Tatton and Hampton Court, before being accepted for the Big Daddy, the annual Chelsea Flower Show at the Royal Hospital in London in May. Jack Dunckley is a good example. At just fourteen, he won a Bronze medal for his first garden at the Malvern Show in 2008, then appeared at the Hampton Court Flower Show in July 2009. In 2013, aged 20, he won a Silver-Gilt medal for his Juxtaposition garden at Chelsea, the youngest-ever designer in the show's history.

The big daddy

The first Chelsea show in 1913 cost £3,365 and made a profit of £88, which was given to gardening charities. Initially, nurseries created the show gardens, and other gardens were made by amateurs for a few hundred pounds. By the late twentieth century, with the media firmly focussed on them, the show gardens had become hugely competitive. Their number increased dramatically, and their cost spiralled into the hundreds of thousands, financed by banks, charities, vineyards and local councils. The entire show has been commercially sponsored since 2000.

Testing the wind - and the designers

Chelsea is a weathervane for garden design, in Britain, at least. Water once played down rock sides, but is now more likely to run along a rusty steel rill, or be trapped within a reflective pool. Functional gardens for modern living, with space for relaxation and entertaining, came to the fore from the 1970s, while in the 1990s there was a mercifully brief appetite for towering palm trees, and stepped terraces of water and plants, as you might see on the roads approaching a Middle Eastern airport. The turn of the twenty-first century saw a mix of cool elegance, created by designers such as Arabella Lennox-Boyd, and sophisticated meadow planting of which Tom Stuart-Smith is the master. Now the emphasis is on sustainability, naturalism and biodiversity, while the Fresh category, introduced in 2012, allows designers to be startlingly innovative.

Beth Chatto's first exhibit caused a style shift in 1976. She went on to win ten Gold medals in eleven years at Chelsea, and paved the way for plantswomen Carol Klein, Rosy Hardy and Jekka McVicar. Their naturalistic planting remains popular over thirty years after Chatto broke the mould, yet still co-exists happily with showy displays of single species, such as lilies, dahlias, roses and sweet peas.

Among the show gardens, the crowd pleaser is always the design full of roses rambling over pergolas, and with beds overflowing with mixed planting and edged with *Alchemilla mollis* and lavender. This, then, is the style which the punters always vote for as the embodiment of English gardening.

Ten facts about Chelsea
– the ultimate garden competition

1. The first show in 1912 consisted of just 244 exhibitors; less than half the number that appeared in 2013.

2. In 1927 there was a campaign to get the RHS to ban foreign exhibits from Chelsea to reduce competition with British firms. The RHS refused saying 'horticulture knows nothing of nationality'.

3. The Great Pavilion at the Chelsea Flower Show is roughly 2.9 acres (11,775 sq.metres) – enough room to park 500 London buses.

4. Of the firms that exhibited at the first show in 1913, three are still showing: McBean's Orchids, Blackmore and Langdon, and Kelways.

5. In 1959, *The Times* was the first newspaper to sponsor a garden, which wowed crowds with its radio-controlled lawnmower.

6.   Each year, the RHS Plant committees vote on RHS Chelsea
     Flower Show Plant of the Year, open to any plant on display
     which has been exhibited at a garden show before.

7.   The biggest Chelsea Show Garden (so far) was the Eden Project
     Garden in 2010, covering 6,351sq.feet (590 sq.metres).

8.   In 2013, visitors to the show guzzled 8,473 glasses of Laurent-
     Perrier champagne, 72,110 cups of tea, coffee and speciality
     coffees, 16,546 soft drinks and bottles of water, 26,363 cakes,
     pastries, muffins and cookies, 4,858 salads and 13,645
     sandwiches, baguettes and bloomers.

9.   It takes 800 people 33 days to build the show from bare grass
     to the finished article.

10. 161,000 visitors attend the show each year.

Record-breaking fruit and vegetables

Longest beetroot, grown by Peter Glazebrook, Nottinghamshire (2010)

21 FEET/6.4 METRES

Heaviest cabbage, grown by Scott Robb, Alaska (2012)

138 LB 4 OZ/62.7 KILOGRAMS

Longest carrot, grown by Jo Atherton, Nottinghamshire (2007)

19 FEET 2 INCHES/5.84 METRES

Heaviest garlic head, grown by Robert Kirkpatrick, California (1985)

2 LB 10 OZ/1.19 KILOGRAMS

Biggest leek, grown by John Pearson, Sunderland (2011)

20 LB 3 OZ/9.2 KILOGRAMS

Largest long gourd, grown by Fred Ansems, Nova Scotia (2013)

11 FEET 7 ¼ INCHES /3.5 METRES

Heaviest onion, grown by Peter Glazebrook, Nottinghamshire (2012)

18 LB 1 OZ/8.2 KILOGRAMS

Heaviest parsnip, grown by David Thomas, Cornwall (2012)

17 LB 3 OZ/7.8 KILOGRAMS

Heaviest pumpkin, grown by Tim and Susan Mathison, California (2013)

2,032 LB/921.7 KILOGRAMS

Heaviest watermelon, grown by Chris Kent, Tennessee (2013)

350 LB 8 OZ/159 KILOGRAMS

CHAPTER 8

WHAT'S IN A NAME?

What's in a name?
That which we call a rose
By any other name would smell as sweet.
WILLIAM SHAKESPEARE (1564–1616)

One of the keenest pleasures for any gardener is rattling off the names of their plants to visiting friends. Most of us delight in the variety and also the sounds of the names, with their underlying associations (about which, more later). It's a great party trick, too, being able to identify a plant in someone else's garden, particularly if you can rap out its Latin name. There are good reasons, however, why it is worth knowing the correct botanical names if you really want to understand your plants.

It began with a rose

Today, there are written descriptions of about 422,000 plants. The journey to the naming of all those plants began around 300 years BCE with Theophrastus, the most important botanical writer before the Renaissance. He got the ball rolling in Athens when he attempted plant classification by identifying both the differences and the similarities between individual plants. He looked, for instance, at the pink and white roses which grew in Greece, and spotted that the flowers, despite basic resemblances, also had their disparities, such as the number and shape of their petals, their colour and fragrance.

Linnaeus and the binomial system

Fast forward to the mid-eighteenth century. In 1753, the professor of medicine at Sweden's University of Uppsala, Carl Linnaeus, published *Species plantarum*. This epoch-making book introduced the binomial system of plant naming, which, after some initial grumbling, has been universally accepted ever since. The system uses two names, like surname and first name, and can be laid out like a family tree. The genus name represents a group of plants with similar characteristics, while the species name represents a sub-group within the genus. There can be hundreds of species within a genus, as a quick glance at the pages devoted to *Prunus* (cherries) in the *RHS Plant Finder* will show. A third name, indicating that the plant is a naturally occurring or nursery-bred cultivar of a species, is written in inverted commas, as in *Salvia involucrata* 'Hadspen'. Cultivars also run into many hundreds: again look in the *Plant Finder* at *Narcissus* (daffodils) or *Rosa* (roses).

Genus (*Salvia*)

(*involucrata*) Species   Species (*nemorosa*)

('Hadspen') Cultivar   Cultivar ('Caradonna')

So why do we use Latin?

Given that the binomial system was dreamt up by a Swede, why isn't the language of botany Swedish, you might ask. Linnaeus's system didn't come out of the blue. Scholars and botanists had been battling with the challenge of classifying a vast new wealth of plant material brought back to Europe over the previous two hundred years by voyages of exploration. And they would have been doing so in Latin, which, until the eighteenth century, was the international language of scholars. Sir Thomas More and Erasmus would have conversed in Latin on the latter's visits to London in the 1520s and 1530s.

So, when Linnaeus looked for names for plants, he automatically turned to the language used by his predecessors. Out of that has developed botanical Latin, which is very different from classical Latin, in that it mixes Latin and Greek. Take the name for a pointy-headed late summer allium, *Allium sphaerocephalon*. Its genus name is Latin, but its species name is derived from the Greek 'sphairo' meaning sphere, and 'cephalon' meaning head. Over the years, other languages have also been drawn in, and transmuted into a kind of cod Latin to reflect changing times.

Not so common currency

Botanical names identify plants precisely and uniquely, and also reveal their relationships to others in a way that common names can fail to. Without knowing the Latin name, you might not realise that the bright red Christmas flower, poinsettia *(Euphorbia pulcherrima)*, is a member of the same genus as the lime-yellow spring flower, wood spurge, or *Euphorbia amygdaloides*.

Maybe that seems like a matter of academic interest, but most plants have several common names, which vary between counties or states, let alone countries, so identification can be difficult. Using botanical Latin means gardeners from all round the world can be sure that they are talking about the same plant. What is mostly called wild garlic *(Allium ursinum)* is referred to in some parts of the UK as ramsons and elsewhere as bear's garlic (a direct translation of its botanical name). The common name for *Achillea millifolium* in the UK is yarrow, but in New Mexico and Colorado it is known as plumajillo (from the Spanish for little feather, because of its leaf shape and texture). The Scots refer to bluebells *(Hyacinthoides non-scripta)* as wild hyacinths. The Americans call *Hesperis matronalis* spring lilac, whereas in the UK it is called sweet rocket or mother-of-the-evening.

Five strange plant names

- **Eastern skunk cabbage**, also known as clampfoot cabbage or polecat weed, is a foul-smelling plant which prefers wetlands (Symplocarpus foetidus).

- **Corpse flower**, so called because it smells like a decomposing mammal. A native of Western Sumatra, its flowering structure reaches to 9 feet (3 metres) above the ground (Amorphophallus titanum).

- **Voodoo lily** is another common name for the corpse flower, but also for the native European dragon arum (Dracunculus vulgaris).

- **Monkey puzzle tree**, or Chilean pine, introduced to Britain in the nineteenth century, owes its common name to someone commenting that 'it would puzzle a monkey to climb that' because of its thick, spiky, symmetrical branches (Araucaria araucana).

- **Devil's walking stick**, a native of America also called prickly ash and prickly elder, owes its name to its sharp, spiny stems and branches (Aralia spinosa).

Latin also makes things neat. Adding the suffix '-etum' to the name of a tree or other plant is an economical way of describing a grove, plantation, garden or collection, as in arboretum (trees), pinetum (pines), quercetum (oaks), rosetum (rose garden) and vinetum (a vineyard).

Making connections

Knowing Latin names helps gardeners to make connections between different members of the same genus. The ebullient, long-flowering bluey-purple climber, *Solanum crispum* 'Glasnevin', is a member of the same genus as the potato *(Solanum tumerosum)*, tomato *(Solanum lycopersicum)*, aubergine *(Solanum melongena)* and deadly nightshade *(Solanum dulcamara)*. That helpful link is a reminder that the flowers of your climbing solanum and the green parts of your potatoes are poisonous, like the obviously evil-sounding deadly nightshade.

The links take you onwards, too, and tell you more about flowers you're considering planting. Another flowering solanum is the all-white *Solanum jasminoides*, which is associated by its species name with the fragrant, summer-blooming *Trachelospermum jasminoides*. Both species names are an indication that their flowers are like those of jasmine *(Jasminum officinale)*, a useful pointer if you're buying the plants out of season.

> *Most convoluted plant name*
>
> *That which we call a daffodil can also be known as:*
> *Narcissus romieuxii* subsp. *albidus* var. *zaianicus_*
> f. *lutescens*

To add to the confusion, there are higher orders of taxonomy: above genus is the family, which comprises many different genera. *Rosaceae*, for instance, includes ninety-five genera, among them *Rosa* (roses), *Malus* (apples), *Alchemilla*, *Sorbus*, and, the largest, *Prunus* (cherries), with over 430 species. But again, the use of Latin makes the links: all members of the *Rosaceae* family are flowering plants.

Helpful pointers

Getting to know your Latin is also a quick guide to whether or not a plant will work in your garden. Look out, for instance, for species names of countries, to see whether the plant's habitat is likely to be cold, hot or sub-tropical: *africanus* (Africa), *americanus* (America), *australis* (Australia), *canadensis* (Canada), *canariensis* (Canary Islands), *hispanica* (Spain) and *hollandicum* (Holland), to name but a few.

Seasonal names tell you when the plant flowers: *hyemalis* (winter), *veris* (spring), *aestivus* (summer) and *autumnalis* (autumn), as in *Eranthis hyemalis* (aconite), *Primula veris* (cowslip), *Leucojum aestivum* (summer snowflake) and *Colchicum autumnale* (autumn crocus).

The most useful species names are those which give fairly precise indications as to the growing conditions the plants require. These include *montana* (mountain), *alpinus* (alpine), *pratense* (meadow), *sylvaticus/sylvestris* (shady woodland) and *aquaticus/aquatale* (water).

How are plant names chosen?

One Greek legend has it that Narcissus was so beautiful that he fell in love with his own reflection and drowned in a pool of water. Another suggests he faded away for love of Echo, whom he'd earlier ignored, and was metamorphosed into a flower. These legends may or may not explain why narcissi are so called, although its spring glamour reflects that of the gorgeous youth, immortalised by painters, sculptors and writers. Its common name, daffodil, is believed to derive from 'affodell', a variant of 'asphodel' (a flower which grew in the Elysian fields) with the Dutch definite article 'de' added.

This explanation hints at the difficulty of being sure how most plants have acquired their names. Common names are often associated with the look of the plant, such as love-lies-a-bleeding *(Amaranthus caudatus)*, with its blood-coloured tassels, or love-in-the-mist *(Nigella damscena)*, with soft-edged flowers and feathery leaves.

Many species have been named for the Europeans who either found them or introduced them from the Americas, Asia or Africa. Examples include the Douglas fir, introduced by David Douglas from Vancouver in 1827, although named in Latin after Archibald Menzies, who had described it thirty or forty years earlier *(Pseudotsuga menziesii)*; and *Hypericum forrestii*, a type of St John's wort, named after another Scottish plant collector, George Forrest (1873–1932).

A few genus have actually taken on botanists' names, although not necessarily because they themselves were responsible for finding them. What seem like Latin words are often, in fact, the Latinising of someone's name. Examples include dahlias (Anders Dahl, an eighteenth-century Swedish botanist), forsythia (William Forsyth, an eighteenth-century royal gardener) and camellias (Georg Joseph Kamel, a Jesuit botanist in the Philippines in the late eighteenth century).

Nurserymen are fond of naming cultivars after their friends and relations. Virtually every member of the family of leading rose-grower David Austin is commemorated by a rose, including his wife, daughter and sister.

It's in the stars

At every Chelsea Flower Show, there's a celebrity photocall on one of the rose-growers' stands, for anyone who is anyone will have had a rose named after them. The list is endless: from TV and light entertainment, look out for Anna Ford, Angela Rippon, Rick Stein, Alan Titchmarsh and Cliff Richard. Musicians are there, too, including James Galway, and the late, great Jacqueline du Pre. Luminaries from the past have their own roses, including Christopher Columbus, Christopher Marlowe, William Shakespeare, Lord Byron, Charles Darwin and Charles Rennie Mackintosh. The royal family are honoured, of course, both gardeners (Prince Charles and Queen Elizabeth the Queen Mother) and non-gardeners (Prince Regent, Princess Alexandra and Princess Anne). And roses, like rosemary, can be on occasion for remembrance. Poignantly, the actress Vanessa Redgrave appeared at Chelsea 2011 to launch Harkness's new pink, scented, floribunda rose in memory of her daughter, Natasha Richardson, who died in a skiing accident in 2009.

Twenty Latin words every gardener needs to know

aestivus..summer flowering

altissimus..very tall or the tallest

aquaticus......................................growing in or near water

autumnalis..autumn flowering

foetidus..smelly

fragilis..brittle

fragrantissimus..very fragrant

frigidus..growing in cold places

glutinosus..sticky

grandiflorus..large flowered *hyemalis*...flowering in winter

lanceolatus..spear shaped

nudiflorus.......................................flowering on bare stems

pendulus..hanging

pratensis...meadow-growing

pungens...sharply pointed

macrophyllus...large leafed

sylvaticus/sylvestris.................growing in shady woodlands

veris..spring flowering

vulgaris..common

Honoured plantsmen
Genus geniuses

Buddleia	Adam Buddle (1660–1710), English botanist
Camellia	Georg Joseph Kamel (1661–1706), Moravian Jesuit botanist
Clarkia	William Clark (1770–1738), American explorer
Dahlia	Anders Dahl (1751–1789), Swedish botanist and student of Linnaeus
Davidia	Father Armand David (1826–1900), French Vincentian missionary and naturalist
Forsythia	William Forsyth (1737–1804), Scottish botanist and royal gardener
Fuchsia	Leonhart Fuchs (1501–1566), German physician and botanist
Lobelia	Matthias de l'Obel (1538–1616), gardening writer and botanist
Tradescantia	John Tradescant the Elder (c.1570–1638), English gardener and plant collector
Wisteria	Caspar Wistar (1761–1818), American physician and anatomist

Species stars

Clerodendrum thomsoniae	Thomas Thomson (1817–1878), Scottish naturalist
Crocus tommasinianus	Muzio Giuseppe Spirito de Tommasini (1794–1879), Austro-Hungarian politician and botanist
Hypericum forrestii	George Forrest (1873–1932), Scottish botanist and plant hunter
Iris aucheri	Pierre Martin Remi Aucher-Eloy (1792–1838), French pharmacist and botanist
Limanthes douglasii	David Douglas (1799–1834), Scottish plant hunter
Magnolia fraseri	John Frasier (1750–1811), Scottish plant hunter
Magnolia wilsonii	Ernest Wilson (1876–1930), English plant collector
Rosa banksiae 'Lutea'	Sir Joseph Banks (1743–1820), English botanist, naturalist and patron
Trachycarpus fortunei	Robert Fortune (1812–1880), Scottish plant hunter, botanist and traveller
Viburnum farrerii	Reginald Farrer (1880–1920), traveller and botanist

CHAPTER 9

THE LANGUAGE OF FLOWERS

Some flowers spoke with strong and powerful voices, which proclaimed in accents trumpet-tongued, 'I am beautiful, and I rule'. Others murmured in tones scarcely audible, but exquisitely soft and sweet, 'I am little, and I am beloved'.

GEORGE SAND (1804–1876)

'Say it with flowers,' went the old Interflora advertisement, the implication being that flowers speak louder than words. We are familiar with the association of red roses with romantic love, of lilies with purity, and red poppies with the annual November remembrance of the war dead. But centuries ago, our ancestors were much more alive than we are now to the symbolism of a host of other plants. Shakespeare, Milton, Marvell, Wordsworth and Keats, to name but a few, all wrote about gardens and flowers, using them to represent different aspects of human experience.

How Ophelia saw it

A good starting point is one of the most famous speeches about flowers in English literature: Ophelia's mad lament in *Hamlet* after the Prince of Denmark has killed her father, Polonius.

> *'There's rosemary, that's for remembrance… And there is pansies, that's for thoughts… There's fennel for you, and columbines – There's rue for you, and here's some for me – we may call it herb of grace o'Sundays – O, you must wear your rue with a difference. – There's a daisy. – I would give you some violets, but they withered all when my father died.'*

In the play, Ophelia hands flowers to various characters for whom each flower's symbolism is appropriate. She unpacks one or two of the allusions, but leaves the people watching her to draw their own conclusions about the rest. Fennel stands for flattery, which the king, Claudius, would receive from his courtiers. Columbines (or aquilegia) are short-lived spring flowers, unpopular in Shakespeare's England, and therefore associated with faithlessness in love. Rue symbolises sorrow and repentance (as witness the verb 'rue', to be sorry for), and was also used in religious ceremonies for cleansing the afflicted. Telling Gertrude to wear hers 'with a difference' points the moral that Ophelia is a sorrowful innocent, while the queen is an adulterer, possibly complicit in her first husband's murder. Daisies represent deception in love affairs, an attack on Hamlet who has betrayed Ophelia's trust, which is why violets, symbols of faithfulness, are not in her sad posy.

In just six lines, Shakespeare compresses many aspects of human life, as well as lining up the main themes of his most famous play. Over four hundred years later, we need the message spelled out to us, but, in his day, the symbolism would have been crystal clear to his audience.

The rose

An ancient and cross-cultural image of love and beauty, the rose has been used in countless ways by many different societies, and by poets, lovers, religious writers, artists and political parties.

In ancient Rome, a wild rose was placed over the door to a room in which secret discussions were taking place, the origin of our phrase 'sub rosa'. The rose was also identified with the goddess of love by both the Greeks (Aphrodite) and the Romans (Venus).

In Christendom, as in Islamic countries, the rose was always given pride of place in gardens, and was endowed with religious and secular symbolism. In Sufism, the rose was associated with the blushing lover and also with divine attributes, while in Christianity the five petals of a single rose were taken to represent the five wounds of Christ. Later, the red rose would come to symbolise the blood of Christian martyrs.

One of many flowers associated with the Virgin Mary, it appears frequently in Medieval religious poetry. In one thirteenth-century 'Hymn to Mary', for instance, she is described as a 'Rosa sine spina' (a rose without thorns). Elsewhere, she is seen as 'moderes flur' (the flower of motherhood).

The Tudor rose is a composite of two roses, with the outer red petals encircling the inner white ones. Devised by Henry VII, it represented the peace and unity he had brought to England by marrying Elizabeth of York. But it also shows the victory of the Lancastrians (the red rose) over the Yorkists (white).

Elizabeth I used the iconography of roses in many of her portraits. She is almost always seen with the heraldic hybrid Tudor rose, but also with eglantine, the only native English rose, to demonstrate her single-minded, virginal devotion to her own country.

The connotations are not always positive. In 'O Rose, thou art sick!', one of William Blake's *Songs of Experience*, the flower has been attacked by an 'invisible worm' (probably a sexually transmitted disease), which has destroyed the lover's 'bed of crimson joy'.

Different coloured roses and their meanings

Pink........................*Grace*
Red..........................*Love*
White.....................*Unfamiliar with love*
Yellow.....................*Infidelity*

Love

'My love is like a red, red rose,' wrote Robert Burns in 1794. The red rose has long been a symbol of romantic love, which is why shops fill with bunches of them in the run-up to St Valentine's Day on 14 February.

But it's not the only flower associated with romance. Camellias, evergreen shrubs native to Asia, are also ancient symbols of love, with the pink camellia denoting longing, and the red, burning passion.

As the name suggests, forget-me-nots represent true love, while orange blossom, the staple of many a wedding bouquet, signifies fertility and happiness. Honeysuckle, gardenias and carnations all have their romantic resonances. Ivy, whose tenacity defeats many a gardener, represents fidelity and wedded love.

Love has its seasons, represented by nature. In another medieval poem, a lover laments as he courts his reluctant lady: 'Al I falewe so doth the lef, In somer when it is grene' ('I fade as does a leaf in summer when it is green').

Kate Middleton's country garden
bouquet for her 2011 wedding

Lily-of-the-valley..............Happiness and purity
Lilac.................................Youthful innocence
Myrtle.............................Hope and love
Field maple....................Humility and reserve
Hornbeam......................Resilience

Consider the lily

The white lily is another wedding favourite, symbolic as it is of chastity and virtue. In Renaissance paintings of the Annunciation, by painters such as Fra Angelico, the Virgin Mary is depicted submissively greeting the Angel Gabriel's message either holding a white lily or with a single bloom in a pot at her side.

Lilies, seen in Cretan wall paintings dating from 1580BCE, were revered by the ancient Greeks, who believed they sprouted from the milk of Hera, the queen of the gods.

Different types of lily have different meanings. The Peruvian lily, or alstroemeria, denotes friendship and devotion; the white stargazer lily, sympathy and the pink stargazer, wealth and prosperity. The white lily is also the flower for May birthdays and thirtieth wedding anniversaries.

The American poet Emily Dickinson wrote often about the lilies in her own garden, asking readers to 'Consider the lily'. In 'Through the Dark Sod – as Education' the lily is a metaphor for the development of the soul.

Passion flower

So-called because it was invested with Christian connotations from its first European discovery in the early seventeenth century. Spanish monks found the exotic flower in Mexico, and sent back drawings to Europe, where in Rome Giacomo Bosio, a monastic scholar, saw them as symbols of Christ's passion. He equated the five stamens with Christ's wounds, the three styles with the nails, and the five sepals and petals with the remaining ten apostles.

Friendship and courtship

The Victorians showed particular interest in the language of flowers. This was sparked partly by the introduction in the 1700s of floriography from Ottoman Turkey, by the traveller, Lady Mary Wortley Montagu. Floral dictionaries were published, and, primed by these, courting couples would exchange small posies, or 'tussie-mussies', loaded with covert messages.

The English word for the large flat-faced viola – pansy – comes from the French *pensée*, or thought. Traditionally, pansies were given by friends on parting to show that they would remain in each other's thoughts.

In 1575, the Earl of Leicester's last-ditch attempt to win the hand of Queen Elizabeth I was to have an elaborate new garden created at Kenilworth Castle. Its impact was partly derived from the language of its flowers, whose rich symbolism would have been immediately intelligible to the queen and court. They were all chosen to emphasise Leicester's status and the magnificence of Elizabeth. Bay, the garland of champions, was used for hedges and topiary, while the roses included *Rosa gallica*, the Apothecary's rose, and the Lancastrian symbol. *Lilium candidum*, the Madonna lily, and symbol of the virginity Leicester presumably wanted to take, also appeared in the garden as a compliment to the queen.

War and peace

'How vainly men themselves amaze, To win the palm, the oak, or bays', wrote Andrew Marvell in the turbulent middle years of the seventeenth century. It is a poem in praise of the garden as a retreat from the horrors of war. Its opening lines spell out classical connotations. Palm branches were awarded to victorious athletes in ancient Greece, while the tree itself came to personify victory in Rome. The oak was sacred to Zeus, the rustling of its leaves in his oracle interpreted by priests. Bay was the symbol of the highest status in ancient Greece, and, again, a symbol of victory in Rome.

Winners continue to be crowned with these three plants, and the terminology is still used. Gaining success is often described as 'winning your laurels', although it is in fact bay, as Marvell wrote. (Bay's botanical name is *Laurus nobilis*; what we think of as laurel is *Prunus laurocerasus*, the beloved plant of Victorian shrubberies). The winner of a motor-racing Grand Prix was decked with a bay garland until the 1980s when commercial sponsorship wanted the lion's share of publicity. But the leaves still appear as a logo on the podium caps handed out to winners. One of the major races at Epsom is The Oaks, and the top film at the annual Cannes Film Festival in May wins the Palme d'Or.

In the Bible after the Flood, Noah dispatched a dove, which came back to the ark with an olive leaf in its beak. The olive tree became for evermore the symbol of peace, and we still use it metaphorically when we talk about trying to stop a quarrel, by 'putting out an olive branch'.

Political emblems

Flowers have always been political emblems. The rose is England's national flower, and is also used by the British Labour party, along with many other social democratic parties across Europe since the Second World War. The oak is the symbol of the UK Conservative party, the National Trust and the Woodland Trust, and of the Basque country.

Each American state has its own flower: bluebonnet or wild lupin in Texas, rhododendron in Washington, the magnolia in Mississippi, goldenrod in Nebraska, and the philadelphus in Idaho.

The fleur de lis, the symbol of France, was used by Frankish monarchs from the time of Charlemagne. Despite the literal translation of the French as lily flower, the fleur de lis (which is also the symbol of Florence) is, in fact, a stylised version of the little wild iris, *Iris pseudacorus*.

The garden of life

Seasons in the garden are like seasons in human life. The greening up of the garden in spring represents the vigour and vitality of youth, the bare branches and snow of winter the melancholy of old age. Think of the Christmas carol, *The Holly and the Ivy*. In it, the winter berries of the holly represent Christ's blood, its prickly leaves his crown of thorns, and the bark the cup of gall he had to drink.

The very fragility of flowers is often used as an image of the transience of human life, as in the fifteenth-century poem by John Lydgate: 'All stant on chaung, like a midsomer roose' ('All life is transient like a midsummer rose').

But then, each year, from out of the bare ground spring forth first snowdrops, then daffodils and tulips, followed by roses, and life is renewed. The words of an Easter hymn seem to sum it up: 'Now the green blade riseth from the buried grain, Wheat that in the dark earth many days has lain.'

Fifteen poems about gardens and flowers

The language of flowers

Here are a few commonly accepted floral interpretations – although you'll notice that some flowers have more than one association.

angelica .....

bluebells .....

carnation .....

clover .....

crocus .....

daffodil .....

forget-me-not .....

gardenia .....

honeysuckle .....

ivy .....

mimosa .....

tulip .....

..... inspiration; encouragement

..... **consistency**

..... affection; health and energy

..... **good luck (especially the four-leafed clover)**

..... cheerfulness; riches (probably because of the
cost of saffron, the stigmas of Crocus sativus)

..... **vanity (because of Narcissus); new beginnings**

..... true love

..... **joy; refinement**

..... happiness

..... **fidelity; wedded love; friendship**

..... chastity; fragility (because of its delicate blooms)

..... **declaration of love**

CONCLUSION

A society grows great when old men plant trees whose shade they know they shall never sit in.

GREEK PROVERB

Gardening unites so many different aspects of human experience: the physical, the spiritual, the intellectual and the social. It is an interest that can be shared whatever your level of experience: professional gardeners will gratefully accept tips from novices. Few painters, philosophers or politicians would be similarly open to such suggestions.

But every gardener will tell you that the more you learn, the more you realise how little you know. Gardening is an inexhaustible subject, a feast of enjoyment for both the initiate and the uninitiated through every season.

I hope that this book will have encouraged you, if not to take up a trowel yourself, at least to go garden visiting. With just a 'little Latin', like Shakespeare, you can enjoy all those intriguing and informative plant names. Indeed, their meanings may suddenly dance into focus, evoking the romantic and even dangerous histories of the plants before you.

And gardening is healthy exercise: a recent Swedish study showed that regular gardening can cut the risk of heart attack or stroke, and prolong life by as much as thirty per cent among people over sixty.

After all, a garden, whether it's yours or somebody else's, offers the promise of constant pleasure and annual regeneration, while the symbolism of its plants, if we're attuned to it, create a deeper, richer experience. It is also a gift for the future. Who could ask for more than that?

GLOSSARY
OF TERMS

Allée
a straight, formal avenue of trees, such as limes

Annual
a plant which completes its life-cycle, from germination to seed-ripening, in one year

Arbour
a bower or shady retreat

Biennial
a plant which takes two years to complete its lifecycle, flowering and ripening seed the second year

Carpet bedding
the patterned planting of fast-growing annuals or bulbs in beds to create a temporary, seasonal display. Particularly popular in the Victorian age, but also to be seen in municipal parks

Cloche

a portable glass dome for protecting plants from animals and the weather

Cloud-pruning

Japanese-style of pruning, which involves clipping trees and shrubs into shapes which resemble clouds

Dibber

a short, pointed tool, almost always wooden, used for planting seeds (and one of the most ancient of tools)

Espaliers

trees (generally, fruit trees) trained, usually against a wall or fencing, with one vertical stem and several tiers of horizontal branches

Genus

taxonomic rank, above species and below family, representing a group of plants with similar characteristics

Ha-ha

a concealed ditch to stop sheep and deer getting into the formal garden, but makes them look as though they're grazing there

Herbaceous perennial

a plant which loses its stems and leaves at the end of the growing season, but lives for more than two years

Herbal
an old-fashioned term for a plant directory

Grafting
a propagation technique by which the tissues of one plant are inserted into the rootstock of another

Parterre
a formal garden, laid out with geometrically arranged beds, often edged in box and with gravel paths between them

Patte d'oie
avenues of trees branching out radially in the shape of a goose foot

Pleaching
the interweaving of tree branches horizontally both for decorative effect and to give support, along an allée or an avenue, usually at head height or above; also used to give strength to hedging

Potager
an ornamental kitchen garden

Rill
small ornamental canal or rivulet, framed usually by stone or stainless steel

Species
taxonomic rank, below genus; plants within the same species can reproduce with each other

Specimen trees
small trees, such as acers, sorbus and prunus, planted individually

Stepover
miniature espaliers, used as ornamental bed edging and ideal for smaller gardens

Stumpery
a garden similar to a rockery, only created using dead tree stumps, logs, branches, and even railways sleepers, and usually planted with moss and ferns

Topiary
the pruning of trees and bushes into fanciful or formal shapes

ACKNOWLEDGEMENTS

My research has been supported by many people. Particular thanks go to Brent Elliott and the librarians at the Lindley Library for their help on this project, as on others in the past. I also want to thank my editor, Anna Martin, for her skilful, light touch, my copy-editor, Jacqui Sayers, for her eagle eye, and Claire Plimmer for commissioning me to write the book. My husband, Chris Evans, as ever, gave me invaluable support, but I dedicate this book to my late father, Norman Berridge, who first inspired my love of gardening.

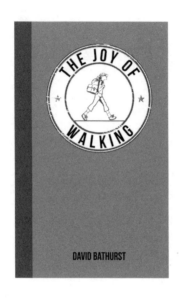

THE JOY OF WALKING

David Bathurst

ISBN: 978 1 84953 553 3

Hardback

£9.99

An early-morning walk is a blessing for the whole day.

HENRY DAVID THOREAU

This pocket-sized miscellany, packed with fascinating facts, handy hints and captivating stories and quotes from the world of walking, is perfect for anyone who knows the incomparable joy and freedom of lacing up your hiking boots and heading for the hills.

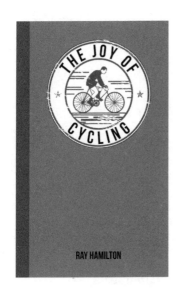

THE JOY OF CYCLING

Ray Hamilton

ISBN: 978 1 84953 457 4

Hardback

£9.99

Be at one with the universe. If you can't do that, at least be at one with your bike.

LENNARD ZINN

This pocket-sized miscellany, packed with fascinating facts, handy hints and captivating stories and quotes from the world of cycling, is perfect for anyone who knows the incomparable joy of bikes.

If you're interested in finding out more about our books,
find us on Facebook at **Summersdale Publishers** and
follow us on Twitter at **@Summersdale**.

www.summersdale.com